Can you pass this safety quiz?

Question 1: What is better than yelling "Help!" if you are in trouble and want to attract attention?

Question 2: Should you put your groceries or your child in the car first? Which is the right choice—and why?

Question 3: Where is the only safe place to stand in an elevator? What should you do if you are attacked there?

Question 4: If you are attacked, it is hard to know whether to fight back or not. What are the 3 situations when you are almost **always** better off fighting back immediately?

Question 5: What is the most important thing your child should know for personal safety? No, it's **not**, "Don't talk to strangers."

Question 6: Why **shouldn't** a single woman put just her initial and last name on her mailbox?

Question 7: When you check into a hotel, which are the safe floors to stay on—and for what reasons?

(***Turn the page for the answers.***)

Answers to the safety quiz:

1. Yell "Fire!" More people will pay attention.

2. Consider putting the groceries in the car first, not your child. You don't want to be standing there with a bag of groceries, while someone steals your car with your child inside. However, make sure your child doesn't wander off while you are loading the groceries.

3. Stand near the control panel in an elevator so you have options if trouble starts. If in danger, hit all the buttons and get out fast, or hit the emergency button and yell your head off (it usually activates a communications system).

4. You are almost always better off fighting back immediately: (1) if someone is trying to take you to a more secluded place, (2) if someone is trying to physically restrain you with rope, tape, etc. or (3) if someone is trying to kill you. In the first and second situations, you are in the best position to defend yourself initially then you will be afterwards. The last situation is obvious.

5. The most important thing you can tell your children is that there is safety in numbers. They should never wander off by themselves—or go with someone they don't know and get separated from the group they are with.

6. These days everyone knows that an initial and last name means a woman is living alone. Better to list your name on your mailbox as "The Smiths."

7. The safest floors are floors 2-6. The ground floor is unsafe because of easy access by burglars. Most firefighting equipment can't reach above the sixth floor in case of fire.

Other important tips in the pages that follow...

What the experts say about

Protect Yourself and Your Family from Crime and Violence

Protect Yourself is, without question, the best and most comprehensive book available on personal safety... This book should be required reading for every woman: business professional, college coed, housewife, and the elderly...an excellent guide for women on how to act, and what to do and say to prevent crime and keep volatile situations under control.

John R. Moore, Executive Director
National Police Officers Association of America

Protect Yourself is a wonderful source of information and tips to help parents teach children personal safety... As a recent victim of an armed robbery, I believe the practical advice offered in this book would have proved very helpful in averting the injuries received during this attack.

Patricia Palmer, Program Coordinator
Children's Resource Network

A terrific book...has a lot of great safety tips that aren't well known... *Protect Yourself* shows that information can be better than a loaded gun...that women don't have to be vulnerable... chapters on driving, work, and entertainment are particularly useful to women of the 90s...

Judith O. Mueller, Executive Director
The Women's Center

All too often, it seems that people in general want to believe that "crime can't happen to me," when in fact we know that crime can happen to anyone... *Protect Yourself* does an excellent job of providing women with the information they need to avoid sexual assault, and is a very positive step toward personal safety.

Kari A. Graf, Rape Crisis Center Coordinator
Women Against Rape

Protect Yourself is a practical, reader-friendly guide to safety which thoroughly covers all aspects of women's busy lives, from concerns about safety in a parking lot, for children at malls, to elevators in convention hotels. Particularly helpful are the Key Points to Remember and Practice Scenarios which appear at the end of each chapter. With more women in the workplace than ever before, chapters addressing safety at work, travel issues, and safety against sexual assault are particularly relevant. This book gives business women useful tips to counter real-life scenarios which may threaten us all.

Leslie Smith, Associate Director
National Association for Female Executives

I feel that the book touches, with great accuracy, all the elements of personal safety for women...we would encourage not only women, but all citizens to read *Protect Yourself and Your Family from Crime and Violence*.

Domingo Herraiz, Executive Director
American Crime Prevention Association

Protect Yourself AND YOUR FAMILY from Crime and Violence

Gerri M. Dyer, Editor

Foundation for Crime Prevention Education
Safety Press / Rockville, Maryland

Library of Congress Card Catalog Number 97-91180
ISBN: 0-9648903-1-3

Cover Design Foster & Foster
Illustrations Tim Martin
Printed in the United States of America

Published by:
Safety Press
Rockville, MD

Disclaimer of Warranty or Liability

This book was written for those interested in crime prevention and personal safety. It is sold with the understanding that the Foundation is only providing suggestions. The information presented is based on many hours of research, but it cannot be assumed that every acceptable crime prevention procedure is contained in this book. The book is designed to complement and supplement other texts and crime prevention sources provided in the Bibliography.

Although every effort has been made to ensure the accuracy and completeness of this information, this book should be used only as a guide to crime prevention. Each situation is different, and individuals must decide their own appropriate actions and reactions when confronted with criminal activity. Readers are referred to their local law enforcement agencies and crime prevention officers as the definitive resources for advice on crime prevention methods and legal considerations.

The Foundation and publisher make no warranty of any kind, expressed or implied, with regard to the instructions and suggestions contained in this book. The Foundation is not engaged in rendering legal advice, and individuals must ascertain and abide by local, state, and federal laws regarding self defense and the use of weapons and/or other protective devices. The Foundation and publisher specifically disclaim any responsibility or liability for any loss, risks, or damages, personal or otherwise, which are incurred incidentally or as a consequence, directly or indirectly, in connection with the use and application of any of the contents of this book.

Organizations and company names are given for informational purposes only. These references do not represent any endorsement, or implied endorsement, on the part of the Foundation or publisher for any commercial enterprise or the products of that enterprise.

Contents

Dedication

This book is dedicated to the memory of the men and women of our police departments throughout the nation who have given their lives in the line of duty, protecting our safety.

Acknowledgments

The development of this book would not have been possible without the support and expertise of many people. Focus group leaders from different regions of the country were: Paula Bryant, Evelyn Cooper, Denise Evans, Tammy Frickx, Irene Horowitz, Beth Ladner, Mary Jo Marine, Monica Perro Cornacchia, Debbi Plitnick, Cathy Simmons, and Taloria Stevenson. Telephone surveys to determine the safety issues most critical to women were conducted by Women Research Associates. Additional technical support was provided by Steven Dyer and Karen Clink. Kerri Jennifer and Elizabeth Chase contributed their unique perspectives to the chapters on child safety. Editorial management was provided by Gerri M. Dyer.

The refinement and enhancement of the final text is directly attributable to the reviewers who took time from their own demanding careers to provide feedback and helpful comments on improving the book and readily shared their expertise on the topics addressed: Peter Banks, National Center for Missing and Exploited Children; Agnes D. Beaton, National Association of Women Highway Safety Leaders, Inc.; Harold Hedley, Child Protection Center; Domingo Herraiz, American Crime Prevention Association; Kay Hollestelle, The Children's Foundation; Kari A. Graf, Women Against Rape; Steven C. Matthews, Montgomery County Police Department; Judy Mueller, The Women's Center; John R. Moore, National Police Officers Association of America; Patricia Palmer, Children's Resource Network; Leslie Smith, National Association for Female Executives; and Rosalind Wiseman, Woman's Way.

Preface

Experts agree that you are much less likely to become a victim of crime if you are aware of potential dangers and are prepared to prevent them. That is the theme of this book. If you and your family understand what you can do to protect yourselves, then violent crime, actually crime of all kinds, could be dramatically reduced.

Communities may call to put more police on the street. Police protection is a critical element of crime prevention. However, the police cannot be everywhere, all the time. That is why people must take responsibility for their own personal safety and teach their children to do the same. You can learn to rely on yourself and intelligently avoid situations that put you in jeopardy. You can be much safer by following the advice in this book, and that will go a long way toward protecting you and your children from crime.

The Foundation for Crime Prevention Education is dedicated to preventing crime with information. This book was written to address the issues of greatest concern to women across the country as determined through telephone interviews. Then, the content and presentation were tested by getting the reactions of many women from different age groups and walks of life. However, the common sense approach to personal safety presented in this book can benefit anyone living in a violent society.

Much research went into writing this book. The advice given has been gleaned from many sources, both from consumer publications and scientific journals, as evidenced by the selected bibliography presented at the end of the book. The information is presented in a format that is easy to read and understand. There are safety tips on subjects that you may not have thought about before.

Reviews of the book by police and women's and children's groups—those that actually understand the dangers women and children really face every day—have been overwhelmingly positive. The dangers are out there, whether a person wants to worry about them or not.

Unfortunately, it is the people who do not want to know about or worry about potential dangers that are at the very highest risk.

This book may seem to contain a lot of information, but that information is important and could save your life someday. The scenarios may be distressing, but the examples presented in this book are far from the most violent crimes that happen far too often.

The purpose of the book is not to frighten you, but simply to make you less vulnerable. However, to do that, you have to be able to approach life with a realistic understanding of the dangers. You also have to be armed with the information that empowers you to protect and defend yourself in a variety of circumstances.

By familiarizing yourself with the topics presented, you can be considerably safer. If you become more aware of your surroundings and prepare yourself as if something bad could conceivably happen to you, and not just to someone else, you will be more alert and careful. That is what being safe is all about.

No one can guarantee that readers of this book will never be the victims of crime. Violent encounters, random assault, rape by a stranger or even an acquaintance, can still happen. However, the chance of bad things happening to you or your family can be dramatically reduced.

That is what we hope for—for you to be safer at work and at play, and to be able to make life safer for your children. There is an old European saying, "live and be well." It is the goal of the Foundation, and the purpose of this book, to make that saying a reality for you in America today.

Foundation for Crime Prevention Education

1

Aware and Prepared

Carla loaded her six children, ages 3 through 11, into the family van to take them to school. She reached for her purse. Not there. She had left it on the kitchen table. She thought, "I'll just dash in to get it. It will only take me a minute." She told her oldest child to watch the others. She left them alone to go back into her house to get her purse. Just as she was coming out the door, in a single moment, a man on the street jumped into the van and sped off with her children, leaving the mother screaming on her doorstep. The man was driving wildly, and a few minutes later he crashed head-on into another van coming down the road. Then, as quickly as he had appeared, the man jumped out of the damaged van and fled on foot. Four of her children were injured in the crash.

Prevention is Power

No woman—or child—is totally safe from crime and violence. Just being in American society, especially in the 1990s, involves some degree of risk for becoming a victim of crime. You can reduce your risk—in fact, reduce it a lot—by empowering yourself with information and following some simple rules of common sense. By becoming "aware and prepared," you can learn to deal with dangerous situations and avoid that "single moment" when you become the next victim.

One *Newsweek* poll found that "fear of violence" was the first concern of parents and their children in cities and towns across America. In President Clinton's State of the Union address in January 1994, he said, "Violent crime and the fear it provokes are crippling our society..." Another CBS Television poll also showed crime as the Number 1 issue concerning Americans.

Women may feel particularly vulnerable to crime. This affects their sense of self and the way that they live. But women **do not** need to be easy targets, and they **do not** have to feel helpless in the face of alarming reports on crime. **Prevention is your best defense**. Being armed with the right information can be better—much better—than a loaded gun.

Crime can happen any time, any place, and to anyone, but you are more likely to be a victim when you are alone and isolated. In a society where the police and courts do not have the resources to keep up with the criminals, you need to accept the fact that your safety is your responsibility.

By being aware, by avoiding danger, and by taking appropriate action, you can greatly reduce your chances of being a victim. Some common-sense precautions can go a long way toward ensuring your personal safety and the security of your family members.

Take Charge of Your Safety

There are several things you can do which will greatly increase your safety and security and that of your family:

- Familiarize yourself with the crime prevention methods in this book—and make sure your family members know them too.

- Discuss how each of you can protect yourselves from crime as you go about your daily routines.
- Practice and rehearse different situations and your reactions to them so that you can "imprint" safe behaviors in your mind and gain confidence in dealing with potential threats.
- Stay aware of the types of crime being committed in your neighborhood by reading your local newspaper.
- Join with others in your neighborhood and be a partner with police to form a united front against crime. Do not hesitate to contact law enforcement agencies about suspicious situations.

Crime in the 1990s

We live in a society where violence is commonplace and crimes occur often. Violent crime has more than doubled over the last 30 years. An American is six times more likely to be assaulted with a weapon today than in 1960. There are more than 200 million guns owned by Americans—almost one for every man, woman, and child in the country.

According to the Federal Bureau of Investigation (FBI), someone in this country is murdered, raped, assaulted, or robbed every 16 seconds. The U.S. Department of Justice reported 10.9 million violent crimes in 1994, with 9 murder victims per 100,000 people.

There were nearly three times as many property crimes as violent crimes the same year. For every 1,000 households, there were 54 burglaries, 18 motor vehicle thefts, and 236 property thefts.

Crime in the 1990s is often related to the illegal drug traffic and the availability of guns, especially to the most criminally active age group of males 16 to 25 years old.

Juvenile criminals come from all social and economic levels. However, they are most likely children who were neglected or abused by parents, come from broken homes, have alcoholic or criminal parents, live in poor housing areas, did poorly in school, and lack training and work skills.

They are growing up in a society where the average American child will have witnessed more than 8,000 murders on TV, many of them shootings, before leaving elementary school. Some of these children are unable to separate "real" from "make believe."

All of this is both sad and tragic for these youths. It also means that it is increasingly dangerous for you to go about your daily life—shopping at the mall, driving your car, walking on the street. It also means it is more difficult to protect your children from harm.

In fact, there is so much news about crime and violence that you may end up feeling fearful all the time or trying to block it out altogether. Fear and anxiety might seem reasonable responses to newspaper and television reports of the latest mayhem, but such emotions take their toll on your sense of well-being and freedom to enjoy life.

The other extreme of ignoring the risks or assuming that crime could never happen to you is not realistic. More importantly, that attitude will increase your chances of being a likely target.

There are two critical ingredients to every crime: the desire to commit the crime and the opportunity to do it. If you can learn to **eliminate the opportunity**, you can go far toward safeguarding yourself against criminals and minimizing your risk of becoming a victim.

Understanding Criminals

Since no two individuals are alike, there is no such thing as a "typical" criminal. Regardless of the motivation or type, the criminal has two main goals—to commit the crime and to get away.

There are professional criminals who consider crime their line of work. There are desperate criminals who are driven by a need for money to obtain food or drugs. Others commit crimes to impress their friends or win approval in gang activities. Still others, and these may be the most dangerous of all, are driven to prove their power over others by abusing, injuring, or killing their victims.

Your primary goal in personal safety and crime prevention is to avoid danger. If you are attacked, though, the way you respond can either help or hurt your situation. If you can, you need to try to understand your assailant to be able to determine the best course of action.

If you are dealing with someone who is nervous, panicked, angry, or under the influence of drugs, failure to cooperate or even to respond quickly enough may increase the chance of a violent reaction. You also need to determine whether your attacker is after your personal property only or intends to do you bodily harm. If you are in physical danger, you need to know some techniques to help you to protect yourself and to escape.

In our culture, women are raised to be polite, cooperative, and caring—hardly the training necessary to identify and protect themselves from dangerous situations. Openness and trust, feeling dependent on others for protection, and a lack of experience in dealing with physical force make women vulnerable to crime.

But women can become savvy and street smart. They can exercise their will and their intelligence, and they can teach their children to do the same. Anything less than that means they are "at risk" of setting up themselves and their families to be part of the crime statistics.

If you are going to be aware and prepared, the first thing you have to realize is that the criminals who would make you their victim do not have the same value system that you do. When you are shocked by the senseless brutality of a particular crime, it is because you cannot imagine how one person could do such a thing to another.

Whether smart or stupid, neat or sloppy, personable or withdrawn, the criminal is anti-social. You cannot expect conscience or compassion from someone who does not respect others. Begging and pleading will do you no good and may escalate the violence. You need to remain calm when confronted by a criminal.

Most criminals are repeat offenders and will continue to perpetrate crimes until they are caught. If they have remorse, it is usually only for themselves on being apprehended. Many will return to crime when they are released from prison and they may have refined their skills and learned some new ones from their cellmates in the process.

First and foremost, **a criminal is an opportunist looking for an easy target**. The best way to avoid having to deal with a criminal is not to be that easy target.

Crime Resistance

The following approaches are effective in reducing your risk of victimization:

- **Be aware of your environment.** Try to avoid areas that are known to be high crime or have gang activity. If you are new to an area, you can check with local police on where the danger zones are. When you travel, you should seek out the safest routes and avoid taking shortcuts that might put you at risk or leave you stranded in deserted areas.
- **Stay alert to your surroundings.** People that are, or even look, confused or preoccupied are likely targets. Use all your senses to assess your situation and trust your instincts. If ever you feel something is wrong, it

probably is. Do not wear headphones; if you cannot hear a would-be attacker, he has the advantage.

- **Take a confident stance.** Walk with a purposeful stride and keep your head up. Make eye contact without being confrontational. Speak in a clear, commanding voice. Attitude is everything. If your body language or voice makes you seem helpless and vulnerable, you are more likely to be victimized.
- **Create obstacles.** If a criminal has too many defenses to overcome, expects to be slowed down, or have attention focused on his actions, he is more likely to look for an easier situation and another victim.
- **Mentally rehearse your options.** It is impossible to practice every scenario or prepare for all dangerous situations, but you can visualize a fair amount. When confronted by a criminal, many people freeze. They freeze because they have never "thought through" what they would do in such a situation.

Mentally preparing yourself to face danger is a powerful technique. You need to condition yourself to take appropriate action, whether that involves quick compliance, ready escape, or lifesaving defense tactics.

Play the "what-if" game with yourself and your children. If something does happen to threaten any of you, you will have already considered your options.

Thinking through what you would do in a variety of situations before you are ever confronted is the best preparation for dealing with crime. That is why several "what-if" scenarios are presented at the end of each chapter in this book for you to consider. Only you can decide the most appropriate response.

This book can help you better understand proven methods for preventing crime and protecting yourself and your family. Reading it is a positive first step for safeguarding you and your loved ones.

However, no one person can fight crime alone. You also should look for other ways and organizations to help in safety preparedness. Get involved with law enforcement and civic associations as well as local schools to sponsor crime prevention forums or action plans to help make your community a safer place to live, work, and play.

Key Points To Remember

- Criminals are opportunists looking for an easy target.
- Stay alert and be aware of your surroundings.
- Look confident and move with purpose.
- Trust your instincts and avoid dangerous situations.
- Mentally practice your responses for crime prevention.
- Join with others and your local law enforcement agencies to make your neighborhood safe and secure.

Practice Scenarios

What If... ?

You are walking down the street and you see three youths hanging out at a corner at the next block.

You go into a parking lot and a man is slouching between two cars in the row where you are parked.

An unfamiliar car is slowly cruising up and down the road where you live.

2

Street Smarts

Jimmy was in serious condition following a car accident involving several teens. That was all his mother could think about as she parked on the street outside the city hospital where he had been admitted. When she walked back to her car after visiting him, she did not notice the youth that approached her from the side. In a flash, she was pushed hard as he yanked her purse from her hands. She fell to the ground, painfully breaking her fall with one hand. Now she had no money, no driver's license, and no keys to her car. But she did have a fractured wrist. Little did she know when she came to the hospital that she would be needing treatment herself.

Out and About

Whenever you go out, take three things with you: caution, suspicion, and realism. You need to be careful, to evaluate what is going on around you, and to anticipate that someone might try to victimize you. For example, laundromats or laundry rooms in multi-unit complexes can be a prime crime location, so take along a friend.

You should map out safe routes and decide on good places to seek help along the way, if you need it. Check out the locations of police and fire stations, hospitals, restaurants, grocery stores that are open late, service stations, and pay telephones.

Consider the type of clothing you wear, not only because of the "appearance" you might present to a criminal who is looking over people as potential targets but also in terms of your ability to escape or defend yourself in case of attack. Flashy, expensive jewelry is an advertisement for robbery. Overtly sexy clothing is certainly not going to help you escape notice, especially by the wrong element. You will cover a lot more distance in comfortable walking shoes or low-heeled pumps than in open back sandals or spike high heels. A tight skirt will limit your mobility much more than a flared skirt or slacks.

Avoid known trouble spots. When you are in an unfamiliar area, put yourself on extra alert. Get directions from a police officer or security personnel so you know the best pedestrian route and you will not appear lost or confused. If at all possible, avoid being out on the street at night alone. If you are, use well-lighted and heavily traveled streets. Do not take shortcuts through parks, school yards, playgrounds, parking lots, or alleys.

If all these precautions seem like "a real bother" or "too much trouble," consider just how quickly you can go from a pleasant evening to real danger for yourself or a loved one. It has happened, just that way, to many women.

Walking Around

When you are walking on the street, you need to appear calm and confident and look as though you know where you are going. This is not the time to daydream or get preoccupied with a problem at home or at work. Since you are at greater risk whenever you are alone, try to have a companion when you go out. If you own a dog, take it with you on a leash.

Try to stay in the middle of the sidewalk, away from doors, alleys, and bushes. Use store windows as mirrors to reflect what is going on around you. Be alert to someone jumping from between parked cars or entranceways.

Brief contacts with strangers in public places may be harmless exchanges, but treat them with a no-nonsense attitude in case the other person is a criminal trying to size you up. Assess the situation and be on the alert if someone continues to approach you instead of moving away after you have answered a question about time or directions. Maintain your distance and keep moving. Never stop or go near a car to respond to a question from either the driver or a passenger.

You have the right to set boundaries. A good rule of thumb is to keep someone else more than an arm's length from your body in any direction. You are less likely to be harmed if someone is not allowed to get any closer than that. Guard your physical space as a precaution.

You can step away from someone who is getting too close to you when walking down a street. If someone seems to be matching steps with you, you can consider doing this: stop, move away, do a quarter turn, and watch him as he goes by.

If he continues to approach you, put your arm out in front and say, "Stop right there. What do you want?" in an authoritative voice. If he still comes toward you, say, "Stop. Go back." You can use a similar approach when dealing with panhandlers or street people if you live and work in a city or are traveling. Keep moving briskly and say, "No. Stand back. Not today."

These techniques of "boundary setting" are not risk free. They may startle and anger some men because they are confrontational. However, these approaches have worked for many women as self-protection techniques and they are explained here as a type of verbal self-defense you could use, if you need it.

If you think someone is following you, switch direction or cross the street. Head toward a place where there are likely to be other people. If you are in danger of being attacked, yell "Fire!" rather than "Help!" That will get you more immediate attention from others.

Never go to your home if you are being followed and there is nobody there to help you. You are safer on the street than you would be in an enclosed space like an elevator or your home with an assailant. Also, if the criminal is after you and not your property, you are showing him exactly where he can get to you at a later date.

Check around you before entering or leaving an elevator. Once on the elevator, stand near the control panel. Do not get on if you will be alone with one or more men that you do not know. If anyone enters an elevator who makes you uncomfortable, get off immediately or at the next floor. Using stairwells in buildings or parking garages can pose similar dangers. See if you can get someone to accompany you—either others who are at the same activity or security personnel, if available.

Always walk facing traffic so that you can see approaching cars. **If you are ever being followed by someone in a car, turn around and walk quickly or run in the opposite direction than the car is heading.** The driver will have to stop and turn the car around, and that gives you a chance to escape. Get the license plate number and a description of the car, if possible, and report it to the police immediately.

Avoiding Street Robbery

The most frequently committed personal crimes are crimes on the street—muggings, purse-snatchings, and pick-pocketing. These crimes may be committed by individuals or teams of two or more people, and the accomplices may often be women.

Muggers use force or threat of violence to get what they want, so many of them have weapons. They prefer to get their victims alone and in secluded locations, and they often grab their victims from behind, forcefully searching for valuables, yanking jewelry from arms, hands, ears, and around the neck. They may hit or push the victim and then flee.

Do not fight or argue with a robber who is only after your purse or other valuables. Hand over what the mugger wants quickly. If you are slow to respond it may be viewed as resistance and could escalate a property crime to a violent encounter.

If you live in a city where street crime is common, you should always carry some "mugger money" on you—at least $20 to $30—to satisfy the psychotic or drug-crazed criminal who might just as soon kill you if you have no cash. If someone robs you, try to commit details to memory so you can describe the criminal and the direction in which he fled. Notify the police immediately, providing as much information as you can about the robbery.

Purse-snatchers and pickpockets can be any age, and the younger ones are more likely to be able to dash away quicker. Once they remove the valuables, they usually discard the purse or wallet. They may simply snatch a purse or briefcase away from the person or cut the strap with a razor or knife, and sometimes the victim may be injured if a struggle occurs. Talented thieves might bump into you, lifting your valuables as they apologize, or have an accomplice divert your attention.

There are some precautions that you can take to reduce your chances of being a victim, but do not tangle with robbers of any type and do not chase after them. They could turn on you with a weapon.

For one thing, do not carry a purse unless you have to. Consider a waist pack worn in front or a small wallet in your front pocket. If you do carry a purse, never keep all your money and valuables together in it. Have some emergency money in a pocket so you can phone for help or pay cab fare if your purse is stolen. An inside coat pocket is a good choice.

Some women sew one in for this purpose. For the same reason, it is a good idea to keep your keys separate from your purse.

If you do not have large sums of money or expensive jewelry on your person, then they cannot be taken from you. You also should not leave your purse open so that money and valuables can be seen, or leave it unguarded on a bench or in a shopping cart. If you are carrying other items or packages, carry the purse between your body and these items.

When walking, carry your purse close to your body towards the front with your hand over the clasp or under your arm. If it has a shoulder strap, wear that securely over the shoulder with the flap facing your body and your arm resting across the top of the purse with your hand firmly holding the base of the strap.

Do not hold the bag with a "death grip." That will only call attention to a potential thief that you have "real valuables" inside. Do not dangle the bag from the strap, either. That makes it easy for a purse-snatcher to grab and run. Avoid wrapping a purse strap around your wrist or arm; you might be injured when the snatch occurs. You should carry a purse or briefcase on the side of your body that is nearest the traffic, but beware of thieves on bikes or mopeds.

If your purse is stolen, you will need to immediately cancel any credit cards, phone cards, and money machine cards, and close the checking account if checks were included. Always keep at least one credit card at home. That way you will have one you can use while replacements are obtained for stolen cards.

You will have to replace your driver's license and any other important documents such as health plan cards. Keep a list of these numbers at home. If your purse contained a social security card, contact the nearest office of the Social Security Administration and obtain a new number. If home or car keys were in it, you will also need to change the locks. If an address book was enclosed, notify your friends and family. Any of these items could be used for setting up other crimes.

Accepting Rides

You should never accept rides from people you do not know or even people who are brief acquaintances until you know them well enough to trust them. Never hitchhike—this practice is so dangerous that you are asking for trouble, and the people that pick you up are more likely to expect sex in exchange for the ride or mean to do you harm rather than be Good Samaritans.

If you find yourself in an emergency situation where you must accept a ride from someone, choose another woman, an older couple, or a family with children. If a friend drops you off near your home or you take a cab, have the driver wait until you are safely inside before driving away.

Jogging and Bicycling

If you walk, jog, or bicycle for exercise try to find a partner and vary your routes so your path is not predictable each time. Avoid trails or paths where attackers could hide. It is better to do any of these activities in daylight, rather than at dusk or in the dark.

Carry some form of identification with your name, address, and an emergency contact number in case you have an accident or are injured. Bring some money so you can make a phone call or take a taxi, if necessary, and do not forget some "mugger money."

There is safety in numbers so try to stay where others jog and cycle. However, keep in mind that criminals can wear jogging suits and ride bikes, so stay on the alert, especially whenever anyone comes up alongside you.

Keep your bike in good working order. If you have a flat or other mechanical problem in a deserted area, walk your bike to a more populated area or a service station before you attempt to deal with the problem. If someone cuts you off, get off the bike from the opposite side. If you keep the bike between you and the other person you can use it as a barrier or shove it at the other person and run, if you need to, preferably along a route that would be difficult for someone on a bicycle to follow.

Bicycle theft is on the rise, so do not leave your bike unattended. Although today's upscale bikes can retail for $500 to over $3,000, they are frequently stolen and cut up to be resold to aluminum recyclers for a few dollars or exchanged for drugs. Bike-jackers often threaten riders with knives or guns. Your best bet is to take the precautions previously mentioned, but if you are attacked, your life is worth more than the bike. If you have an expensive model, make sure it is covered by your insurance policy, so it can be replaced if stolen.

Gang Violence

As the number of street gangs increases, so does the level of violence on the street, as members seek attention, fight over turf, and challenge each other on drug deals. Many rival gangs go after each other with drive-by shootings. There has been a sixfold increase in juvenile gang killings from 1985 to 1993. You can either be singled out as a target, if you are in "the wrong place at the wrong time," or you or a family member just might get caught unintentionally in the crossfire.

Avoid going into areas where there is known gang activity. If you live in an area where gangs are the norm, know the players and stay out of their way. If you see a group of young men hanging out together, do not plan on walking their way.

The same can be said of a car full of youths; duck into a store or other public building until they pass. If you are ever on the street when shots ring out, drop down to the ground immediately and seek cover. The lower you are, the less likely that a bullet will find you. Then get out of the area as soon as it is safe.

Key Points To Remember

- Plan a safe, direct route and stick to it.
- Do not wear restrictive clothing or flashy jewelry.
- Stay on busy, well-lit streets at night.
- Walk in the middle of the sidewalk.
- Set boundaries and keep a safe distance from strangers on the street.
- Walk facing traffic so you can see approaching cars.
- If you are being followed, change directions and head for other people.
- Be especially cautious in elevators, stairwells, and garages.
- Do not resist street robbery; give up your property and get away.
- Always carry emergency money and keys separate from your purse.
- Never accept rides from strangers or people you do not know well.
- When you jog or bike, vary your route, bring company, and choose populated paths.
- Avoid high-crime areas and gang activity.

Practice Scenarios

What If... ?

A man asks for directions and then keeps walking alongside you.

You are walking home from a movie and you think you are being followed.

A car pulls up and the driver says, "You better get in this car now."

Someone grabs your purse and starts dragging you into a doorway.

You are at a party and a friend of your girlfriend offers to drive you home because your place is on the way to his apartment.

You are jogging on your favorite trail and a man jumps out from the bushes and blocks your path.

3

Shopping and Entertainment

It had been a great day of shopping, thought Eleanor—fabulous sales—as she pushed open the exit door, her arms full of packages. She looked all around the parking lot, not sure where her car was. She finally spotted it—farther out than she had realized when she parked earlier in the day. She did not notice the man behind the van on the row where she parked. She was too busy looking in her purse for her keys. As she pulled the keys out, she felt a sharp point in her side. "Give me your keys," the man said, pushing the knife deeper. Eleanor drew in her breath. How could this be happening to her? This was the parking lot of a big mall. The man opened the door and pushed her in. He drove to a secluded spot only 10 minutes away. He raped her, took her purse and car, and left her sobbing along the side of the dirt road. All she could think about was who was going to pick up her children at the bus stop?

Mall Madness

Criminals like to hang out at shopping malls—shoppers are easy victims, especially when they are distracted or loaded down with packages. Women with small children can be ideal targets when their attention is diverted. As in many other situations, bringing another adult along when you shop or run errands will reduce your risk of being a victim.

Shopping malls are also ideal locations for people intent on harming children who get separated from their parents. Keep your children with you at all times, and make sure they understand not to stray. Under no circumstances should you leave them unattended in stores, entertainment arcades, or theaters. It only takes a few seconds to grab and abduct a child, even though there is just a small chance that this will happen.

You should never let a child use public rest rooms alone—these are favorite locations for people who would harm children. Even adults need to be wary when they use public facilities, especially if the rest rooms are in out-of-the-way areas or down deserted corridors. Stay on guard and if anything does not seem right or there is a group hanging out near the doors, turn around and get out of there quickly. Find more suitable facilities elsewhere.

It is highly unlikely that you would be personally assaulted while in a busy store, but a thief can use the crowds to provide cover for a quick getaway after taking your valuables. While there is always some chance that you might be endangered if an armed robbery occurs while you are in a store or perhaps a bank, the greater risk is in the parking lots surrounding the mall, especially if there is a highway nearby or the mall is in a high-crime area.

Always try to park as close to the mall or store entrance as possible, and lock your car. If a mall offers valet parking, use it, especially if you are alone. If you have to use a parking garage or deck, park on the level that gets you directly into the mall. You could be accosted in elevators and stairwells. Stay alert to people standing between or behind parked cars or large pillars in garages, as well.

If you are shopping at night or late in the day so that it might be turning dark by the time you leave the mall, park in a well-lit area, directly under a light, if possible. If you are alone at night, go to mall management and ask that a security guard accompany you to your car.

Do not park next to or between vans or trucks; not only will they limit the sight of the area around your vehicle, but they could also harbor muggers or even rapists waiting for a likely target to come along. If you come out of the mall to find a large vehicle parked next to you, be on the alert.

The best location in a large parking lot is at the end of a row, and make a note of the parking spot. If you are confused about your car's location when you return with packages in hand, wandering around the lot in search of your vehicle, you are a prime candidate to be a victim. You may want to tie a colored ribbon on the antenna to make your car stand out from the others.

Have your keys in hand and walk purposefully to your car, looking around to ensure a clear path. Do not put packages or your purse on top of your car. Quickly put your purchases in the trunk or take them into the car with you, first checking to see that nobody is in the car. Then lock the doors as soon as you are in.

If you are purchasing bulky items, either have someone go with you, ask the store to hold the items for you until you can get someone to help you pick them up, or have them delivered to your home. Struggling with large purchases puts you at a major disadvantage in defending yourself against theft or attack.

If you are on a shopping trip where you will buy several items and will need to move your car from one location to another, try to arrange it so your most expensive items are purchased last. Also place all items purchased in the trunk of your car, if at all possible. Items that are visible through car windows, either on the seats or floor, invite theft. If your car does not have a trunk, such as with a station wagon or hatchback, hide the items purchased under a cargo cover or blanket.

If you have your children along with you when you shop or run errands, **never leave them alone in the car**, no matter how short a time you think you will be away. Children have been accosted while parents dashed in to a convenience store to get milk or return a video rental. If you are getting out of your car to pump gas, make sure to take the keys with you and lock the doors. A carjacker can jump in an unlocked car and take off with your children inside while you stand there with gas pump in hand.

Watch Your Purse

You need to pay special attention to your purse when you are out shopping or socializing. Do not put it up on a counter while you are paying for something or walk around with it half open. That makes it too easy for someone to grab your wallet while you are preoccupied. Do not sling it over a chair when you are seated or leave it on the floor or table—the best place is in your lap.

When you use a public rest room, put your purse on a purse shelf if a protected one is provided in the stall; otherwise place it behind you on the tank top or keep it in your lap. If you put it on the floor or hang it on a door hook, someone outside can grab it by reaching under or over the stall partition. Also, do not forget to take your purse with you when you leave.

If you are clothes shopping and using a dressing room, be careful where you put your purse as well. Just as in a rest room, a thief can reach under or over a partial door or through a curtain to grab your purse from the floor or lift it off a hook. Never leave valuables in a dressing room if you go out either to look in a mirror or to find additional clothing items to try on.

Credit Cards

Americans lose millions of dollars each year due to theft and credit card fraud, so safeguard your credit cards. **Never give out an account number unless you are initiating the charge.** Cut up expired cards (and pre-approved credit applications you receive) before tossing them out.

Immediately report the theft or loss of your cards. Also, notify the issuing company if a renewal card is not received before the expiration date of the card you have—it may have been stolen from the mail. Consider services that keep a record of your cards and, with one phone call from you, will cancel them and request replacements, if they are ever stolen or lost.

Treat your cards as you would cash—most people do not carry around $2,000 in cash, but they may very well have a credit card with a limit of that amount or higher. Keep cards in a secure place at home and only take the card or cards you actually need when you go out for a specific purpose. It is best to keep them separate from your wallet or in your pocket instead of your purse; you are less likely to be wiped out that way in case your purse is stolen.

Credit card numbers from legitimate transactions have sometimes been used to make unauthorized charges to accounts. Always check a sales slip or voucher over carefully before signing to be sure it is completely and accurately filled out. Make sure your card is returned to you along with the customer receipt and the carbon copy, if any. Keep your copies of charge slips and compare them with your monthly statements to see if they agree with the charges listed. Contact the card issuer immediately if the charges do not match.

Keep in mind that merchants across the country routinely violate your privacy rights and credit card company restrictions with their own policies for check and credit card acceptance, and they leave you vulnerable to consumer credit fraud as a result. It is not unusual for a merchant to ask for two forms of identification when you write out a check—your driver's license and a major credit card.

There is nothing wrong with showing your credit card or even noting the type of card (MasterCard, Visa, American Express); the problem comes when the credit card number is written on your check. Or you may be asked to write your address and phone number on a credit card slip. In either instance, key information about you is annotated on a single document that will pass through many hands. Unscrupulous people could use this information to run up charges on your account or set up credit lines in your name for their own use.

Try to resist these practices. Since a clerk will only be following store policy, you may have to talk to a manager. Explain that you do not want to be exposed to credit card fraud.

You may obtain information on your rights as a consumer and privacy and fraud protection by sending a check or money order for $3.00 to: BankCard Holders of America, 524 Branch Drive, Salem, VA 24153 or call 540-389-5445.

Money Machines

An Automated Teller Machine (ATM) is a fixed location where people go to get money—anyone can figure this out—so although it is a convenience to have 24-hour-a-day banking, you need to understand the attraction that these money machines have for anyone with a drug habit, a bad attitude, or a weapon. Use a cautious approach and never proceed with a transaction if anything looks suspicious.

Park as close as you can to an ATM, or better yet, find a drive-through station so you do not have to get out of your car. Whether on foot or in your car, look over the ATM to be sure nobody is lurking around the area before using it. The best location for a woman alone would be an ATM inside a busy supermarket; this is especially important at night. Keep your card and deposits, if any, in your pocket until you get to the machine.

Be sure to block the view of others nearby whenever you enter your personal identity number (PIN) at an ATM. Never undertake a transaction when others are crowding you in. If someone is hovering, find another ATM location. Also make sure the person in front of you clears away before starting your transaction; it could be someone just waiting for a victim to show up.

Once you complete your transaction, put your money and card away quickly—do not stand around counting your money or rearranging your purse. Wait until you are in a more secure location than on the street. Check to see that you are not being followed; some thieves follow people when they leave ATMs and subsequently rob them when they are in a more secluded location.

When selecting a PIN for a money card, do not use a number that someone else could easily figure out, either by looking at other documents in your purse (such as a social security number or birth date) or by watching you at the key pad (such as 1-2-3-4). Never write the number down where it might be found with the money card. You should memorize the PIN and file it away in a secure place.

Never let anyone else use your ATM card on any pretext or give out your PIN, even if the person claims to be an officer of your bank. Selecting an all-purpose number as your secret code is not a good idea; each money card you own should have a different PIN. Otherwise, if the single code is broken, all your accounts could be cleaned out.

If you are ever accosted at an ATM station, give up the money, and treat it as you would a mugging—your life is more important. If you are ever forced to use an ATM by someone, calmly tell your assailant that there is a daily limit that you can withdraw (usually in the $200-300 range), so he understands you are not holding out on him, and you will give him that amount. The idea is to give him money and get rid of him; then you can report the crime. This is far better than being hurt or killed for resisting.

Public Amusement Areas

Plan entertainment activities with at least one other companion. If you can get a group together, that is even better. Not only can it be more fun, but the more people you have together the safer you are from crime. Criminals know that your guard is down when you are having a good time, but they are much less likely to tackle a group.

Since there is safety in numbers, even when you are alone, stay where there are other people, and do not let someone get you away from the crowd on some pretext. Serial killer Ted Bundy frequently lured his victims away from others by asking for help in carrying something to his car because his arm was in a sling. These women were never seen alive again. If you have to leave a group for any reason, tell someone where you are going and when to expect you back.

Just as it is generally safer on the street during the day, the same thing is true of outdoor amusement areas, beaches, and parks. Evening outings alone are not worth the risk. Even when you are with an organized party, you need to be on extra alert at night. Use well-traveled paths and stay together. Leave valuables at home; expensive jewelry and credit cards are not needed and represent a liability in these settings. You should also put some cash in several hidden locations rather than have all your money in a purse or single pocket.

Since groups that can cause trouble may congregate in these areas, your own party needs to assess the behavior of others. If another nearby group's behavior is getting out of hand or seems menacing, relocate your party elsewhere. There are several cases where confrontations between groups in public amusement areas have resulted in severe injury and death.

Theaters, Restaurants, and Bars

When you are seated in an arena or theater, keep your purse on your lap. Do not put it on the seat next to you or under your own seat; it is too easy for someone behind you to slip away with it. If you go to a movie alone, find an aisle seat next to another woman, a couple, or a family. Also, check to see where the emergency exits are located in case you have to head for one in the event of a disturbance or crisis.

When in restaurants, keep your purse on your lap, rather than on your chair, table, or the floor. If you are going to eat in a restaurant alone, pick a place that has the bar separated from the dining room. A woman eating or drinking alone in a bar is at risk.

The trouble with bars is that they are public places with little control, there are plenty of strangers, you can expect crowds and noise, and people are drinking. The guy you meet may be tall and handsome, but is he dangerous? This is not the place to let your guard down or put your good sense under a hat. Remember, the vast majority of criminals are under the age of 30, and it is the young crowd that tends to frequent bars.

For starters, leave the expensive jewelry, unnecessary credit cards, and excess cash at home. Carry enough cash to get you through the evening paying your own way and assuring you have taxi fare in case you need it. Do not accept drinks or drugs from others, especially people you have just met. Watch your own alcoholic consumption—try nursing one drink through the whole evening or switching to soda or bottled water—alcohol impairs judgment and will affect your responses.

Stay with your friends—do not let anyone talk you into going off with people you have just met for other entertainment. You can be friendly, but not overly friendly. Do not give out personal information or leave identification lying around while you chat or dance so that others can get at it. Keep your valuables with you in a pocket or a small purse with the strap slung diagonally across your chest, or give them to a friend for safekeeping until you return to your table or stool.

If you meet someone that you would like to get to know, do not give out your address or home phone number. Ask for the other person's phone number and say you will call in a few days. You can also suggest that you meet for lunch in a popular restaurant or arrange to meet at some other public place.

Do some homework before getting involved—find out what you can and check out the details of what you are told. Meet again in a public place and bring a trusted friend along for an opinion on your new acquaintance. You need to screen people to reduce your chances of being victimized by either a criminal or an unbalanced person.

Key Points To Remember

- Never leave children unattended at malls or public rest rooms.
- Park close to main entrances, note your parking location, and lock your car.
- At night, park in well-lit areas and get escorted to your car.
- Have large purchases delivered to your home or get help in loading them into your car at the store.
- Do not leave purchases in plain sight in your car; lock them in the trunk.
- Have your car keys in hand and check in your car for anyone hiding there before you get in.
- Never leave children alone in a car while you run an errand.
- Do not leave your purse on store counters or the floor or door hook in a rest room or dressing room.

- Safeguard your credit cards and review all charges. Never give out your number unless you are making a charge.
- Use extra caution at automated teller machines. Choose busy locations and protect your personal identity number. If accosted at an ATM station, give up the money—your life is more important.
- Stay with groups at public amusement areas; do not go off to isolated locations.
- When out socializing, do not impair your judgment with excessive alcohol, and be wary of new people you meet.

Practice Scenarios

What If... ?

You pull into a parking spot at the mall next to an occupied van with several young men in it.

Your child wanders away from you in a store and you see a woman take your child's hand and start heading for the door.

You go down the corridor to the public rest rooms and notice several people standing around outside the door.

You took longer than you thought and now it is dark out and your car is parked in a remote area of the mall parking lot.

You go to make a purchase and realize your credit card is missing, because the cashier at the last store did not give it back to you.

Shopping and Entertainment

You are in your car at a drive-through automated teller machine when you see a man on foot headed your way.

You are at the beach and a distressed man asks you if you can go with him to the bath house to see if his missing daughter is there.

You are at a bar with friends, and a charming man you have been talking with asks you to accompany him and his friends to a party.

4

Car Sense and Security

Cheryl was so excited about her graduation present that she could hardly wait to drive over to her best friend's house to show her the 2-year-old blue metallic Camaro. Once the two young women were in the car, they decided to take the car out on the highway to see what it could do, but first they stopped at a convenience store to get a couple of sodas. They dashed in to grab some "munchies," neither bothering to lock the doors. When they emerged 10 minutes later, the car was gone. But someone else put it to good use, robbing another convenience store on the outskirts of town, before heading the car down an embankment into the river.

Repair and Maintenance

One of the most important things you can do to increase your safety and prevent putting yourself in jeopardy while driving is to keep your vehicle in good running condition so your car does not break down. If "things mechanical" get the best of you, you should take a class or get a friend or family member to go over the basic operation of a car with you.

Let someone show you the typical trouble spots that can cause a car to stop working. Go over the basic fluids that are essential for the running of the vehicle and how to add them to your car—oil for the engine, water and coolant for the radiator, and brake, power steering, and automatic transmission fluids. Sufficient windshield washer fluid is also needed during bad weather conditions. Locate your fuse box and learn how to replace a fuse.

Look over your owner's manual and get servicing done on your car according to the maintenance schedule listed. Always have the car checked over before leaving on a trip. If your car feels or sounds funny, get it in to a mechanic for a check right away. Do not wait until the car breaks down and you are stranded to figure out that it needed servicing.

When purchasing a vehicle, check on the reliability, safety features, and average maintenance costs for the make and model of the cars you are interested in. Your local library can help you find articles and comparisons. The magazine *Consumer Reports* rates the dependability of various vehicles. If you are a single woman or spend a lot of time alone in a car commuting or traveling, this is an important aspect of your overall safety picture.

Before you decide, you might also want to check with local police on the make and model of cars most often stolen in your area; some are more popular with thieves. A hardtop car is more secure than a convertible, because it is easy to rip open the convertible's roof. You are also more vulnerable to carjacking in a convertible when the top is down. Utility vehicles, on the other hand, increase security because they give women a higher vantage point for surveying surroundings.

Sign up with an auto club for emergency repair road service and towing. This type of help is invaluable if your car breaks down; so is a car phone to call for help. Most of these clubs also provide trip planning services. They help members determine the best routes to their destinations, and the clubs provide maps as well as other services and discounts that benefit the traveler.

As obvious as it may seem, watch your gas gauge so you do not run out of gas. When your gas gauge reads half-full, make a stop at a service station and fill up again. Never go below a quarter of a tank. You do not want to risk sputtering to a stop because you could not find a station for a refill in time. Also, in cold weather, you are more likely to get a frozen gas line when the amount of gas in the tank is low. Fill up during daylight hours as much as possible. If at night, choose well-lit stations in populated areas and use the pumps that are most visible from the station office or attendant's booth.

If you do not know already, have someone show you how to change a tire, removing the flat and replacing it with the spare tire. Go through the process yourself a few times to make sure you understand the steps involved, and then actually change the tire. You need to have practice and be comfortable with the process now. Ensure beforehand that lug nuts on all wheels are not too tight for you to loosen.

Waiting until you actually have a flat tire to try dealing with it will leave you unprepared and could put you in a dangerous, even deadly, situation if you are alone on a deserted stretch of road when it happens. Make sure you keep a spare tire, a good jack, and a lug wrench that fits the lug nuts on your wheels in your car at all times.

Watch your car keys when changing a flat. You do not want to accidentally lock them inside your car or trunk because you are flustered about your roadway emergency. Be sure to engage the emergency brake and put blocks of wood behind the rear tires if the flat is up front, or blocks ahead of the front tires if the flat is on the back, before you jack up the car. Otherwise, a car tilted up by a jack may roll and come crashing down on you.

You have two other alternatives in the event of a flat tire. The first is to use a can of "flat-tire fix" that will temporarily seal and inflate a flat tire until you can get to a service station and have an attendant put on the spare tire and fix the flat tire. The second is to drive slowly (5 miles per hour) on the flat tire until you can get to a station for help. You will ruin the tire and the rim of your wheel doing this, but if it is a question of your safety or the added cost of a tire and rim, your safety comes first.

Car Safety Kit

The greatest safety net you can create for yourself and your family in dealing with any and all car emergencies is to put together a "safety kit" to keep in the car at all times. The items you include will depend on your own situation, but you should be well-equipped enough to deal with common car problems, seek emergency assistance, and survive if you are ever stranded in your car.

Check with your dealer or service station on the basic equipment items that fit your car. Many items can be bought at discount auto supply stores as long as you know the model, make, and year of your car, and these stores also have a good selection of emergency road supplies.

Outdoor and camping stores carry emergency food and water supplies with long shelf lives, and you could get survival items there such as a "space age" mylar blanket. You might want to keep your emergency food supply as simple as packaged peanut butter crackers and juice in cartons. If you have children, consider what it would take to keep them comfortable if you were stuck in your car for some time. This might include extra diapers and baby food, if you have an infant, or coloring books and crayons for older children.

A reflective "Please Call Police" sign that you can put in the window of your car may be obtained from the Los Angeles Commission on Assault Against Women. Call 213-462-1281 for ordering information. Another outlet to obtain a reflective sign is from Citizens Against Crime (800-466-1010). You might alert criminals to your predicament by using this sign, but it also gives the many drivers with car phones a chance to call for help on your behalf.

Use the following checklist to build your safety kit:

- ☐ tool kit, including lug wrench
- ☐ spare tire and jack
- ☐ wood blocks
- ☐ pair of jumper cables
- ☐ can of emergency flat tire "air" sealant
- ☐ extra fuses
- ☐ brake fluid, transmission fluid, power steering fluid, and engine oil
- ☐ special tape to repair radiator hoses
- ☐ coolant/antifreeze
- ☐ gallon of distilled water
- ☐ tow chain or rope
- ☐ windshield scraper
- ☐ extra windshield wiper blades
- ☐ white handkerchief or cloth strips
- ☐ reflective "Please Call Police" sign
- ☐ highway flares and matches
- ☐ reflective vest or tape for clothing
- ☐ first aid kit
- ☐ maps, paper, pencil or pen
- ☐ large police-style flashlight
- ☐ blanket
- ☐ fire extinguisher
- ☐ foodstuff
- ☐ child supplies

Auto Theft Prevention

One motor vehicle theft occurs every 20 seconds in this country, and this crime alone costs more than $8 billion each year. Every time a car is stolen that also has the owner's address—and keys or garage door opener—the personal safety of the owner at home is at risk as well.

Sometimes neighborhood youths take a car on a joy ride. If so, they will most likely damage your car with reckless driving before abandoning it. They might even crash your vehicle, especially if they try to escape police who are in hot pursuit. More often though, stolen cars mean professional car thieves are at work.

Most of the vehicles stolen by organized car theft rings are never recovered. Sometimes the vehicles are stolen to be used in the commission of a crime, but it's more likely that they will be sold off in another state or country or dismantled and sold for parts. Do not leave your automobile registration in the glove compartment; that makes it too easy for car thieves to "prove" ownership when they dispose of your vehicle.

In the same way that burglars are often aided by homeowners who leave their doors unlocked, car thieves often have a simple time of it because the car owners do not secure their own property. In four out of five cases of car theft, owners have left the doors unlocked. In one out of five cases, the keys were in the ignition. **You should always lock your car and take the keys with you whenever you get out of the car**, no matter what the location or how brief a time you think you will be. Also, roll up the windows. Make sure all windows are closed, including vent windows.

A car is five times more likely to be stolen from an unattended parking lot than from an attended lot. The longer a vehicle is left in an unattended lot, the more likely it will be targeted for theft. Auto thieves do not like working in areas where there are people.

Some parking attendants could be dishonest and have duplicate keys made, so it is important never to leave house keys with the car keys. Give the attendant the key to your car doors, but not the one to your trunk, if you have a separate key. That way the possessions you store in the trunk cannot be easily stolen. Also, never leave anything in your car that has your home address on it.

Sometimes thieves will leave your car alone and just go after what is in it. Lock up valuables in your trunk and keep them out of view. This would include any packages you have from shopping or errands as well as tape decks, CD players, car phones, and CB radios. If you do not have a trunk, keep items under a tarp or blanket or slip them under a seat if they will fit.

Just as you should mark the valuables in your home, you can engrave your driver's license number and state abbreviation on valuables in your car that are likely to be targeted by thieves—your CD player or tape deck, a car phone or CB radio. In addition, engrave the number a couple of different places on the car itself, such as inside the car door and under the hood. This will help with positive identification if your car is later found after a theft.

Glass etching kits are also available for purchase that allow you to mark your driver's license number directly on your windshield. This might make a car thief decide to pass up your car.

Car Alarms and Devices

Additional protection for your car can be provided by a variety of security devices. You may purchase a car with an alarm system installed at the factory or later purchase one from an automotive supply store or many other outlets. The problem with the factory installed alarms is that they are standardized, and operation manuals are available from dealers. A determined and mechanically inclined thief can buy a manual and use the information to disconnect your system.

Just as you should comparison shop for a home alarm, you need to do the same for an auto alarm to get the features, performance, and cost that fits your situation. Your nearest police station may be able to provide specific recommendations based on your needs, local crime prevention efforts, and any state legal requirements.

Some auto alarm systems have a siren, others activate the horn or lights, and still others include a separate flashing strobe light. Some systems combine these features. The idea is to scare off the thief. Several systems need to be professionally installed, while others are for do-it-yourself installation. Portable models are available that plug into the cigarette lighter of your car. There are key-operated systems, those that use a punch-in code to activate and disarm a system, and some that are operated by remote control.

If you think you would have problems remembering to turn your alarm on and off, there are passive systems that are armed automatically with timed delays to allow you to get in and out of the car. These are usually tied into the ignition system of your car and are activated and disarmed when you remove your key or insert it in the ignition.

Some systems might include motion, vibration, or pressure sensors to set the alarm off if the doors are opened or windows broken, or if your car is jacked up or towed. One way to make it difficult to tow a car is to park with the front wheels turned sharply to the right or left.

Unfortunately, most of us have become so accustomed to false alarms that many people do not pay attention to car alarms. A passerby might assume the owner has accidently set the system off. Few people will risk their lives to confront a thief to save someone else's property. The best you could hope for is that a policeman or security officer might be nearby or might be notified by a concerned citizen of an alarm sounding and the license plate number.

If a thief can choose between a car with an alarm system and one without, he will most likely choose the latter. The main advantage of these systems is that they protect you while protecting your car. An alarm system reduces the chance that someone will break into your car and wait for you there—hiding in the back seat.

A security alarm may deter a thief, and it can alert you that your car is being broken into. However, alarms alone will not stop someone from actually stealing your car. For that, you have a choice of several types of devices that immobilize a car in different ways.

An automatic fuel cutoff prevents fuel from reaching the carburetor. A second ignition switch that is hidden, known as a "kill switch," can stop the electrical current from reaching the coil or distributor unless it is activated. Another system locks the starter so it is inoperable.

Some antitheft systems have multiple cutoffs that make the car almost impossible to start. One system, called "The Immobilizer," has been shown to be effective in deterring theft, and it is available from Quorum International (602-780-5533).

A steering column "collar" is a permanently installed device that can stop a thief armed with only a screwdriver from punching through the lower steering column beneath the ignition and starting a car in less than 20 seconds. Citizens for Auto-Theft Responsibility (CAR) offers theft deterrent collars for many car models (561-478-8990).

One popular item that is affordable and relatively easy to use is called "The Club." For ordering information, call 800-527-3345. This heavy-duty metal bar locks the steering wheel in place and prevents someone from being able to maneuver the car if they tried driving it away. Although a determined thief could cut through your steering wheel, it is not likely that the average thief would be equipped to do so. Another type of device that is available locks the steering wheel and the brake pedal together.

One system that helps police track down and recover your car if it is stolen is called "LoJack." This involves a hidden transponder in your car that would send a signal out if your car is taken. The police in your state would have to be part of the transponder network for this to work, and only selected states are currently part of the network. For additional information, call 800-535-6522.

Two other helpful items to have that add to the security of your car are an interior hood lock and release and a locking gas cap. The first keeps the hood locked to prevent tampering with your car when you are not in it. The second protects your fuel supply; gas cannot be siphoned off or damaging materials, such as sugar or sand, cannot be dumped into your fuel tank.

If your car does not come equipped with these items, you can subsequently get the hood lock installed or replace the fuel cap with a locking one. If you have an expensive car with custom wheels, you should also have locking lug nuts or lockable wheel covers to prevent theft of the wheels.

Since the trunk is where your safety kit is as well as the best place to keep packages and store valuables from inside the car, you should consider having the trunk lock hardened with a heavy-duty antitheft lock and plate. Get a reputable locksmith to do this for you.

Be sure to get several written estimates of any car alarm systems, security devices, or installation work you are considering. Check out the companies before you decide, and make sure the company you use fulfills the written agreement. Ask for the carton that your system was shipped in along with specifications, owner instructions, and warranty. Check with your insurance agent on the security measures you are considering to protect your car; you might be eligible for a discount on your rates.

Keeping Channels Open

A cellular phone can be the best safeguard if you have an emergency; pick a dependable service for your area. More and more people are getting them for their cars, and the majority say it is for safety reasons. People are using them not only for their own safety but to report disabled cars with stranded occupants, drunk drivers, crimes in progress against other people, and suspicious behavior to the police.

A cellular phone is particularly useful to women driving alone. If you have car trouble, you can call for help. If you are being threatened in some way by another vehicle or followed, you can call the police, and just putting the phone up to your ear may be enough of a deterrent to scare off would-be assailants. It is a good idea to program 911 or another emergency number into the phone's dialing memory to speed the process along.

Some car phones are installed and are powered by the car battery. Or you can get a portable phone that plugs into the car's cigarette lighter or runs on a rechargeable battery. You can "hide" it on the floor of your car when you park so it is not a visible target for thieves. Or if it is a smaller model, you can take it with you wherever you go to call for help if you need it. A portable phone can also be brought inside with you at night and do double duty as the emergency phone in your home in the event of a break-in while you are there.

These phones have become more affordable as they have grown in popularity. You can obtain a unit for less than $150 from a discount electronics store and keep monthly charges in the $20-$40 range as long as you reserve use of the phone for emergency purposes only. Like an insurance policy, you hope you never have to use it, but you will be extremely glad that you have it if you do.

Another option, especially in rural areas, is the use of a portable emergency Citizen's Band (CB) radio. Keep it under the seat of your car. The unit usually comes in a carrying case and plugs into the cigarette lighter of your car. The range may not be great, but you can listen to a CB to find out about traffic and weather conditions, and the police, sheriff, and highway patrol monitor Channel 9 which is the distress channel for CB users.

You can also have a regular CB installed in your car, but you should be able to remove the unit and put it in your trunk when you are not driving the car to prevent theft of the unit. An antenna can either be permanent or you can get a magnetic antenna that attaches to the roof of your car when you operate the CB.

Car Information File

Set up a "Vehicle Identification" file card with pertinent information on your car for safekeeping. This card should include the "I.D. numbers" on your car keys as well as the year, make, and model of your vehicle, your vehicle identification number (located on a small metal plate on the dashboard), the license plate number, and the color and other identifying marks that distinguish your car. That way you have all the important information to give police if your car is ever stolen.

Key Points To Remember

- ▸ Understand the basic operation of your car, and keep it in good running condition to avoid breakdowns.
- ▸ Join an automobile club that provides roadside emergency service.
- ▸ Never drive alone when you are low on gas or having car trouble.
- ▸ Know how to change a flat tire and carry a can of flat-tire fix.
- ▸ Put together a basic emergency supply kit to keep in your car.
- ▸ Keep the doors locked and windows closed whenever possible.
- ▸ Keep valuables locked in the trunk or out of sight.
- ▸ Only give the necessary car keys to a parking attendant.

- Install an alarm and other immobilizing devices to deter theft.
- Buy a cellular phone or Citizen's Band radio for emergency use.
- Set up a file card with detailed information on your vehicle.

Practice Scenarios

What If... ?

You are driving home from work and your engine starts making funny sounds.

It is late at night and you have less than a quarter tank of gas as you leave a friend's house to drive home.

You notice that one of your tires looks low, but you only have 5 miles to drive down a back road to get home from the store.

The ice was unexpected and you slid off the road into a ditch; now you and your baby are stuck in the car until help arrives.

You are on a deserted country road and a couple of men in a pickup truck are tailgating you and hollering out the windows.

Your car disappears from the parking lot and you have to report it to the police.

5

Personal Safety and Driving

Christine had dropped her two friends off after attending a party and was heading home. It was nearly 1 a.m., and she had to admit she was feeling tired and did not look forward to the 40-minute drive to her parents' house. She was driving down a back road as a shortcut to the main highway when her car sputtered and stopped. Now what, she thought, I'm in the middle of nowhere! She was so relieved when another car pulled up behind her half an hour later. The two guys that got out had been drinking, but what could you expect on a Saturday night? They offered to give her a ride to the intersection with the highway where there was a truck stop. She could get something to eat there and call her folks. She never made that call.

Selecting Your Routes

Choose the more traveled, heavily populated routes whenever you go on a trip because you are more likely to be able to get help or service if your car has trouble. There is always a risk in using back roads because of the isolation and lack of service stations along the way.

If you use a less traveled route deliberately when you commute to work to reduce the stress of driving in heavy traffic, then notice the places where you could get assistance in an emergency and approximate distances along your route. Are there police or fire stations along the way? Where are pay phones located? What about convenience or general stores where you could stop if you needed help? Where can you get gas?

Know where you are and where you are going. Have up-to-date maps in your car of local areas; obtain maps for other locations when you travel. If you are going somewhere new, go over the maps before you leave home and mentally travel your route. Write instructions to yourself on the routes you will take on a memo pad, giving street names and route numbers, approximate miles, directions, and any landmarks you will pass, so you can keep the instructions with you as you drive. Consulting maps or having them visible in your car tells criminals you are unfamiliar with the area and sets you up as a mark. Keep them under the seat.

An important safeguard is to tell someone where you are going, the route you are taking, and your expected times of departure and arrival. Make arrangements to call this person to check in when you arrive. If you are delayed or never arrive at your destination, then this person could notify police of your expected whereabouts or, if you are in the local area, might go looking for you along your intended route.

If you get lost while driving, either go to a gas station for directions or—much better—ask for assistance from the police or highway patrol. It is not a good idea to stop and ask strangers for help. Not only might they give you incorrect information, you could also be setting yourself up for a crime, especially if you get lost in a bad neighborhood.

Another consideration that can affect your safety and survival is the weather conditions, especially if you are stranded in snow, get caught in an ice storm going up steep inclines or down winding roads, or your car stalls while driving through flood areas that are swollen with rain. Always get the latest weather reports before leaving for your point of departure, your destination, and areas in between. Avoid traveling, or even going out locally, during severe weather.

If you are ever trapped in your car because of inclement weather, it is best to stay inside the car for protection unless the vehicle itself is in jeopardy. If you have put together a car safety kit, you should have the essentials for waiting out the weather and surviving until rescue help arrives.

Parking and Garages

Always park as close as you can to your destination, rather than in isolated areas. Park near main entrances or attended booths whenever possible. If at night, make sure the parking space is well-lit and near a heavily trafficked area. Try to avoid subterranean parking areas or parking decks if you are alone at night. Do not park and leave your car if you think you are being followed, and do not head for home, either. Drive to the nearest police station, fire station, or hospital and report the license number of the car following you.

Approaching Your Car

Do not walk into a parking area with your head down or rummaging through your purse. Get your car keys out while still inside a building and have them in hand. Not only will you be ready to unlock the car door quickly, but a set of keys held firmly in your hand with the points protruding from your fist can be used as a defensive weapon against an assailant. Check to see if there are any suspicious people loitering near your car before you approach it. Do not go to it if there are.

Sometimes thieves or rapists will deliberately disable your car. One way is to flatten a tire. Another is to stuff the exhaust pipe, which will prevent the engine from starting. The distributor cap or battery could be removed if your hood can be sprung from outside, so make sure you have a locking hood. A favorite ploy is to then offer you help with the problem. Look over your car from a distance to see if you notice anything wrong, and go back inside for help if you do.

If you are in your car and it will not start, the best idea is to stay put with the doors locked and windows closed. Then, use your cellular phone or CB radio to call for help. If you do not have either, wait until there are several people in the lot or garage before getting out again to go for help. If you feel you must leave your car, do so only after you have surveyed the area for anyone lurking.

If someone approaches you while you are in your car, speak through the window. Tell the person to get security for you or call your auto service club. If they insist you open the door, lean on your horn or set off a car alarm if you have one—anything to create noise and call attention to yourself.

Always look into your car, especially the back seat, before entering it, to make sure no one is hiding out on the floor. If someone was hiding there and you did not notice, you would be extremely vulnerable. Being held from behind and told to drive, usually with a weapon on you, is a dire situation. The longer you stay captive, the more likely that you will be harmed, and you do not want to be forced to drive to some deserted area where you are really at the mercy of your assailant.

If this ever happens to you, stay on guard for your first opportunity to halt your own abduction while pretending to go along. If he thinks you are cooperating, you may be able to convince him to loosen his hold or put down his weapon. Then you might slam on your brakes at a red light or stop sign and jump out of your car, or drive the car up over a sidewalk on a lawn and lean on your horn—anything to throw your attacker off by surprise and gain attention while you get out of the car and run. You will have to pay for damages, but if it saves you it is worth the cost.

It is always extremely dangerous to be captive in a car with an assailant. Once you drive to a secluded area, he will have even greater control of the situation. **If you are ever approached by someone and ordered to get in a car, always try to find a way not to do it.** Running, screaming, attracting attention in any way may put you at risk, especially if the assailant has a weapon. But getting into the car is a bigger risk.

Avoiding Carjacking Attempts

Carjacking refers to auto theft when the victim is present, and the car is taken from the person by force or threat of force. Unfortunately this crime is on the rise, and it can happen anywhere to anyone. You are vulnerable to carjacking while entering, driving, or exiting your vehicle. Common sites are parking lots, service stations, automated teller machines, convenience stores, and supermarkets.

It is harder to steal unoccupied cars nowadays because of available alarms and anti-theft devices, so the criminals target unsuspecting motorists. A carjacker may want a vehicle for the commission of a crime or to get quick cash, sometimes for a drug habit. More teens commit crimes of violence than ever before, and they might do this even for kicks.

In one case that shocked the nation, a 34-year-old research chemist was yanked from her car at a stop sign a block from her suburban Maryland home while she was driving her 22-month-old daughter to her first day of preschool. In a desperate attempt to get her little girl who was strapped in her safety seat, she was caught in the passenger side seat belt. The carjackers continued driving, dragging her along for a mile and a half before her body fell from the vehicle. Then they tossed the child, still in the car seat, from the car. A witness to the mother's brutal murder rescued the child.

The two Washington, D.C. youths responsible were tried and convicted and are serving life sentences for the carjacking/murder. However, the tragedy for this woman's family and the outrage of decent people over this terrible crime brought the reality of carjacking to the forefront for many people.

If you are approached by a gunman who wants your car, give it up. Avoid confrontations. If you have children with you, make it clear that the thief can have the car, you just want your children out of it first. One technique to consider is to throw the keys away from your car for your assailant to retrieve so that you have a chance to remove your children. Move away quickly from your car; you do not want to be kidnapped along with your car. Call the police immediately and give them a description of your car and your assailant.

Learn to get into your car quickly and immediately lock your doors. Teach your children to do the same. **Get children situated in car seats and seat belts after you are safely inside with the doors locked.**

However, when shopping with children, consider loading the packages or groceries first, then putting your children in the car. This prevents a carjacker from driving off with the kids while you are loading the car.

Always look around you 360 degrees before you unlock your car and get out of it as well. Just staying observant and alert can go a long way to reducing your chance of being a victim. At home, be sure the garage door is down before opening your car door.

A favorite ploy of carjackers on the move is to bump another car from behind as a "fender bender." Then when you stop and get out of your car to observe the damage from this minor accident, you are confronted by an armed assailant who orders you to give up your car and your valuables.

If your car is hit from behind, motion to the other driver to follow you and then head to a public area where you can be seen, preferably a police station, and exchange insurance information. Take down the license plate number of the other car before getting out of your car.

When Driving Alone

Get in the habit of always driving with your doors locked and your windows closed. In warm climates, air conditioning is not only a comfort feature but a safety feature as well. Never have your windows open more than 2 inches for ventilation, especially if you are going to be in stop-and-go traffic in populated areas. Make sure your locks are kept in working order; you can help ensure smooth operation by lubricating them with a product made for this purpose available from an auto supply store.

Stay alert to what is going on around you. Regularly do a three-way scan of your surroundings using the left side mirror, the rear view mirror, and the right side mirror so you are aware of other vehicles and activity on the street other than what you see looking out your windshield and front side windows.

Remember that you are almost always safer in your car than you are out of it, unless it is on fire or something equally dangerous is happening. The car affords you an armor of steel and the chance for mobility and escape as long as it is operating and you stay in control. You are more vulnerable when you slow down or stop.

Never roll down a window when someone approaches your car; speak through the glass and be prepared to take off at the first sign of trouble. Be on extra alert when slowing in heavy traffic or coming to a stop at an intersection. Do not drive next to curbs or median strips in heavy traffic if you can help it; stick to the middle lane in three-lane streets. On two-lane streets, pick the inside lane away from the sidewalk.

Do not keep your purse on the front seat of the car; it is not unusual in cities for thieves to smash the passenger side window and grab the purse and run. Keep the purse under the seat. If someone walks into traffic and jumps in front of your car trying to stop you, consider moving your car forward slowly and carefully and make it clear through gestures that you are going ahead and the person should get out of your way.

Do not tailgate. Try to keep enough space between you and the vehicle in front of you so you can maneuver in an emergency. Always be careful when cars or vans pull up alongside your vehicle; watch for doors opening next to your car or occupants with weapons. If weapons are present, look for an escape—you might drive over a curb, do a U-turn, turn right or left—something unexpected so you can get away. You could also apply your brakes and let the other vehicle overshoot yours. If your erratic driving gets the attention of police—even better—you are less likely to end up a victim.

If another driver harasses you by following too close, cutting you off, racing alongside you, trying to run you off the road, or trying to get you to stop, move out of the way or drop back. Keep driving until you can get to a police or fire station, a service station, a hospital emergency room entrance, a busy shopping area, or somewhere around other people where you can get help or report the incident to the police.

The other driver could be drunk, high, crazy, or intent on making you a victim, so never challenge the irrational behavior and do not stop. Get the license plate and a description of the car and driver, if possible, and notify police.

Never pick up a hitchhiker, not even if you think the person is a stranded motorist. If you see someone in trouble, call in the location to the police at your first available opportunity, but do not stop. There are too many highway rapists—or others willing to do you harm—waiting for a compassionate woman motorist to stop. Some criminals set up false "distress" situations to get unsuspecting drivers to come to their rescue so they can rob them; for example, a woman may be used as a decoy.

If you think you are being followed, make four right turns in quick succession to see if the car behind you does the same, or pull over into an area where there are other people and that is well-lighted if at night, and see if the car continues past you. Under no circumstances should you drive to your home if you are being followed. Head for a police or fire station, a service station, or another area where there are lights and people. Do not get out of your car. Lean on the horn to get attention, if necessary.

Be careful of phony police. A flashing light on top of a car does not automatically make it an unmarked police car. If someone flashes a badge at you through a window and motions you to move over, it does not mean he is a police officer. Do not stop. Motion to him that you see him and will stop. Then drive to a police station or a well-lighted place with lots of people.

Even if you are pulled over by someone who seems to be a legitimate police officer, always ask for his name, his badge, his police identification, and his precinct before rolling down your window. If you have a car phone, call his precinct to verify his badge number against the name he gave you. Not only does this confirm that the officer is on the level, it gives you the added security of reporting your meeting to the precinct.

If Your Car Breaks Down

Whenever you have car trouble, pull off the road enough to be clearly out of the path of traffic, but still seen. If you can get to a service station or a busy parking area, assuming you have power and can steer, that is better than endangering yourself on the roadway. Otherwise aim for the shoulder of the road. Now is the time to put your cellular phone or CB to use in calling for help. If you do not have either, realize that you are extremely vulnerable in this situation and you need to be very cautious to protect yourself.

If your car dies on a highway, there are several ways to signal you have car trouble. Put your emergency flashers on so you can be seen. Place road flares on the highway side so they can be seen. Raise the hood of your vehicle. Tie a white handkerchief to the radio antenna or door handle on the driver's side. If you are near a callbox or public telephone, carry your flashlight and make your distress call.

Do any or all of these things as quickly as possible and then get back in your car and lock the doors; make sure the windows are up as well; if you need ventilation, only roll down the window an inch or two, not enough for someone to shove a hand through.

Once your car is stopped, put it in "park" and turn the engine off to prevent carbon monoxide poisoning. Put a "Please Call Police" reflective sign in your car window where it can be seen by passing motorists. Granted, this advertises your plight and can present a risk, but it also gives drivers with car phones the go-ahead to call for help on your behalf.

If someone stops, ask the person to call the highway patrol for you, but do not get out of the car. Do not fall for the ploy that the person wants you to look under the hood so you can help fix the problem. Once out of your car, you can be dragged behind it out of view of the traffic.

If a car pulls up with one or more men, say that a nice family already stopped and called the police and road service for you on their car phone. You expect one or the other to arrive shortly so there is no need for additional help. Discourage men from hanging around, not only because they may mean you harm but because they may keep others who could help you from stopping or calling for help.

If you are on a back road or in a deserted area when your car gives you trouble, look for a driveway, rather than stopping on the road. At night try to find a home with lights on and occupants. Ask that the homeowners make a phone call for you to a road service, family member, or friend.

Key Points To Remember

- Plan your route in advance and choose well-traveled roads.
- Note locations along the way where you could get emergency help.
- Let someone know your route, destination, and schedule.
- Ask directions from reliable sources, such as the police.
- Avoid driving alone in inclement weather.
- Park close to your destination in well-lit, heavily trafficked areas.
- Approach your car alert and ready to unlock it.
- Check to see if anyone is loitering near your car or is hiding inside.
- Be wary of strangers offering you help if your car is disabled.
- Resist attempts to force you into a car; try to escape.
- Always situate children in safety restraints after you get in the car and lock the doors.
- Be aware of and extra cautious about carjacking ploys.
- Avoid carjacking confrontations; give the car up and get away.
- Drive with your car doors locked and windows rolled up.
- Be on alert at stop signs, traffic lights, and in slow traffic.
- If someone approaches your car, honk your horn and pull away, if possible.
- Keep your distance from other vehicles and always look for an escape route if you are being harassed by another vehicle.

- If you are being followed, head for a police station or other busy area to get help, but do not go home.
- Never pick up hitchhikers or stop for disabled motorists.
- If your car breaks down, try to get off the road enough to avoid oncoming traffic.
- Call for help on your car phone or CB radio, use a highway call box, or put out a distress signal, but wait inside your car with the doors locked.
- If a motorist stops, ask him to send help, but do not roll down your window or get out of your car.
- If you are near a house, ask the homeowners to make an emergency phone call for you.

Practice Scenarios

What If... ?

You are meeting friends at a ski resort that is a 2-day drive for you through new territory.

You are lost and it looks like you are in a rundown neighborhood.

The same car has been behind you since you left the parking garage.

Your car will not start, and a man parked next to you gets out and asks if you will open the hood so he can take a look.

As you go to get into your car at the convenience store, a teen rushes up with a knife and tells you to give him the keys.

As you pull up to the traffic light to make a left turn, a man approaches with flyers in hand and knocks on your window.

You are driving down a side street when the car behind you hits your back bumper, and you notice two men in the front seat.

Your car breaks down on the highway, and a station wagon with a family in it pulls over. The woman in the passenger side gets out and asks if they can help you.

6

Securing Your Home

"I learned all about a home security audit—from the police officers who responded to my call at 2 a.m.," says Anne Marie, age 26, as she describes the burglary of her townhouse. "I returned home from dancing with friends to find my place looking like an earthquake had hit. The officers showed me where the burglars had broken a basement window to gain entry and then unlocked the back door to carry out their haul—my TV, stereo system, camera equipment, jewelry, and whatever cash I had. What bothered me even more than the theft of my possessions was the violation of my living space. Strangers had been there. They had gone through my closets and drawers, including personal items, dumped the contents, and taken what they wanted. They not only left me with a mess but a sense of vulnerability. I still feel uncomfortable about it. New locks on the doors, bars on the windows, and an alarm system can't give me back the sense of security I used to have in my own home."

Burglary Today

If you would like to think of your home as a safe haven from the world, then you need to take some steps to ensure your security there. One burglary is committed every 11 seconds in this country. If you do not think much about home security, it is an open invitation for criminals: "Come on in and help yourselves."

Nearly half of all residential burglaries occur when thieves gain entry through unlocked doors and windows. You cannot afford to be complacent or careless—both the professional burglar and the amateur thief will take advantage of you in either case.

About half of all home break-ins occur during the day, so the typical work hours of 8 a.m. to 5 p.m. are prime "work" time for burglars, too. The only thing worse than a break-in while you are at work or running errands is one when you are at home. Then you can be assaulted or raped also. In fact, one out of three assaults and three out of five rapes that occur in the home are committed by burglars.

However, most burglars prefer to loot your home when you are not there. For one thing, it is safer for them if there is no confrontation with anyone. Also, a break-in of an unoccupied home is a less serious offense than the assault of a resident would be—if they are caught. That is why it is important to make your home **look occupied**, even when it is not.

Unless a criminal wants to tangle with the people inside, he will bypass your home in favor of an empty residence. However, you need to be prepared in either case. There are several things you can do to ensure the security of your home when you are **out** of the house and your own personal safety when you are **in** it.

Protecting Your Home

The steps to prevent residential theft that are recommended by law enforcement officials throughout the country really come down to three basic goals:

- Make your home uninviting as a target for burglary.
- Make it difficult for someone to get inside.
- Protect valuables and decrease the likelihood they will be taken.

If you are going to stop a break-in, you need to burglar-proof your home in a variety of ways. The more layers or levels of security that have to be penetrated, the less likely it is that your potential intruders will take the trouble. Make your home **look secure** on several fronts.

Assessing Your Risk

Look at your home the way a burglar would in sizing it up as a likely target. Most burglars want quick entry and concealment. You need to find ways to slow them down and show them up. The longer that burglars have to spend to get in, the more likely it is that they will be seen.

Research shows that if you can delay entry for a few minutes, chances are the burglars will give up on your home and look for an easier target. Better still, you want to discourage them from even considering your home in the first place.

By examining your home from the perspective of a burglar, you can determine the weak points and fortify your home for better protection. Many local police departments are willing to provide such a security audit of your house. Check to see if a police officer will come to your home and make recommendations on ways to increase your safety there. You can also use the security audit checklist provided at the end of this chapter.

Zones of Safety

When you think about home security, try to imagine three zones of safety. The outermost safety zone is the exterior, the area surrounding your home. The middle zone is the perimeter of your home and includes all points of entry. The inner zone is the interior of your home. It is also the place you will be if someone tries to break into your home while you are there. You need to have a contingency plan if that happens. There are precautions that can be taken to protect your property and yourself in each of these zones.

Your Home Exterior

The condition of your neighborhood can affect your risk. Run-down areas attract crime. Nearby vacant buildings and abandoned cars can harbor thieves while they monitor the activities of residents. Broken street lights provide the cover of darkness for a quick get-away. If you are aware of these factors, you can work with others in your community and local officials to improve conditions.

First you need to assess your home from the street as if you were a criminal casing your home as a potential target. In looking at your particular house within the neighborhood, you can determine how much a burglar can see by answering the following questions:

- Can items of value, in your yard or your home, be seen from the street?
- Are the empty boxes of expensive new purchases, such as TVs or computers, in clear view for trash pickup?
- Is it easy for passers-by to monitor the activities in your home through windows without curtains, blinds, or shades that serve as a privacy screen?

- Does a high wood fence, brick wall, lush landscaping, or poor lighting provide protective cover for a would-be intruder attempting to gain entry?

Yard Security

Security begins in your yard, so consider what kind of impression your grounds make. If you have fences, do the gates have locks that work—and are they used? Store lawnmowers and other equipment in locked buildings. Outbuildings and sheds should have sturdy doors and be secured with padlocks made of case-hardened steel with 3/8 inch shackles (Figure 1). Look for the type that does not release the key until the padlock is locked; this will prevent you from unknowingly leaving it unlocked. For your convenience, you can buy "keyed-alike" padlocks where one key will open all the padlocks in a set.

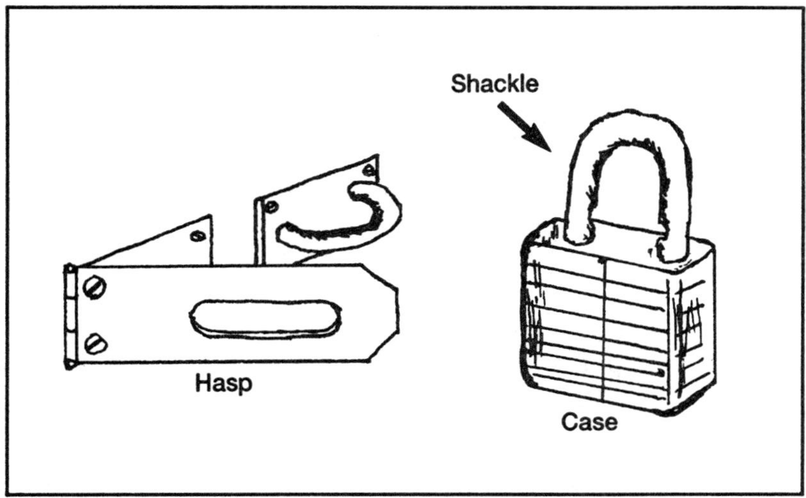

Figure 1. Case-hardened padlock for yard security

Do not leave bicycles out in the yard; more bicycles are reported stolen in the United States than any other single item. If a bicycle cannot be stored in a locked shed, garage, or basement, then secure the bicycle frame to a post with a steel U-bar lock. Also register the serial number of any bike you own with the police so it can be traced in case of theft.

Make sure that ladders or other tools that could help a burglar to break in are kept out of sight and securely locked up. Do not make the criminal's job any easier by providing help for him to break into your house.

Keep your yard in good shape; an overgrown appearance can indicate that no one is home. Prune shrubbery that could provide cover for a burglar, especially around windows and doors. Plant thorny bushes as a deterrent under windows that could be points of entry.

Check outbuildings, fences, porches, decks, fire escapes, and flower trellises to determine if they could be used to gain access to a second story window, balcony, or the roof. If they can, take extra precautions to safeguard these points of entry. If a tree near the house has sturdy limbs that could be used to climb into windows, cut back the limbs or have the tree removed.

Outside Lighting

One area that cannot be stressed enough for the exterior of your home is lighting. Two things are critical for your protection:

- Seeing anyone approaching your home from a distance.
- Eliminating darkened areas or deep shadows where burglars could be lurking or prowling.

Light up porches, entrances, and yards to the front, back, and sides of your house. Install bright floodlights and have them out of reach so the bulbs cannot be removed or easily broken. You can cover the bulbs with protective wire mesh as an extra precaution. A good location is the eaves of the house.

Keep lights on when it is dark. You can use timers or automatic lighting systems that use photoelectric cells to turn lights on at dusk and off at dawn. There are some automatic lights on the market that are powered by solar cells, and these can be a good backup in the event of power outages.

Another type of automatic lighting uses motion-detection sensors. These lights come on when a person walks within range or some other movement occurs. They are particularly useful near entrances. These lights are convenient when you are returning in the evening, and they also may startle approaching intruders who think their presence has been detected by the occupants of the home.

If you have power or fuse boxes outside, secure the boxes with sturdy locks and check them each month to ensure they have not been tampered with. It is also a good idea to protect or hide the outside wiring that leads into your house. Telephone and electric wires can be covered by hardened steel tubing. Or an electrician can bury outside wiring and move utility connectors into the basement, if allowed by your local utility. You want to limit the opportunities an intruder has to interrupt power to your house or cut your phone line.

Clearly display your street address number on both your mailbox and your house. Reflective numbers work best for mailboxes. Ensure that house numbers are visible from the road (6 to 8 inch numbers on a contrasting background are best) and lighted, if possible. This is important for two reasons:

- Others can readily report the number if they see any suspicious activities around your house.
- Police, firefighters, and rescue teams can easily locate your home if called in an emergency.

Your Home Perimeter

Keeping someone outside your home from getting inside is what perimeter security is all about. From the burglar's point of view, the best way to enter a house is to get in without having to force entry. This can be accomplished in two ways: (1) getting in through unlocked windows and doors or (2) using a key. To counter the first, you need to install good locks and then be sure to use them **always**. To counter the second, you need to practice good key control.

Key Control

Poor key control is one of the reasons that burglars are so often successful. One way that a criminal can obtain keys is from a "secret" hiding place around the house—over the door sill, under the door mat, in a flower pot. These "great" hiding places are no secret to the seasoned burglar and they can easily be found by the casual thief as well.

Better to leave a spare key with a trusted neighbor. Identify it with a colored tag, but do not put your name or address on it. In case your neighbor's home is burglarized, you do not want to make it easy for the burglar to get into your home, too.

Another way that your key can fall into the wrong hands is when you leave it with someone providing a service, such as cleaning or repairs. Only do business with reputable companies whose employees are bonded and insured. Carefully screen any people coming into your home who will have access to a key, and consider who might have access to them, as well.

In one case, the son of a cleaning lady "borrowed" the home keys his mother had and made duplicates. While she was working hard to support him, he was working hard to support his drug habit.

In another case, the boyfriend of a babysitter visited her one Saturday night after the children in her care were asleep. While there, he helped himself to a spare key that was hanging in the kitchen. He then returned to the home when the family was attending Sunday worship. Not only could he let himself in, but he had identified the items he wanted the evening before.

Keep spare keys (home and auto) in a secure place in your home that is out of sight. Otherwise, they can be spotted and easily picked up by people who are visiting, making deliveries, or providing household services and repairs.

Never hand over the keys to your house to a parking attendant or for any auto service performed. It is always best to keep house keys and car keys separate. If they are on the same key ring, detach only the car keys needed and keep the rest. Some key chains have two sides that pop apart so you can separate the car keys from your house keys in such situations.

If you have a spare key made, pay by cash—checks and credit cards can be traced to an address. Never attach keys to anything that has your name or address on it.

If any member of the family loses a key, **rekey that lock.** It may be that the key was misplaced; then again, someone else might have stolen it. Reinforce in children that have keys two important precautions: they should never broadcast this fact, and the key should be kept safely out of sight.

Whenever you move into a new residence, rekey or replace all the locks **immediately**. In fact, if you can have the locks changed just before you move in, that will better safeguard your possessions and yourself. There is no way to know who had access previously or how many spare keys were given out by the former occupants. There are numerous instances of families moving into homes only to be cleaned out shortly afterwards with no evidence of forced entry.

Door Security

Keeping your doors locked at all times is the single most important personal safety habit you can adopt. You should ensure that all entrances are locked when you are in your home and you should lock them whenever you step outside or go to a neighbor for even a moment.

One successful burglar looked for residents who were outside their homes working in their gardens; he usually entered through an unlocked back door.

Another disturbing crime occurred one summer evening that was later reported by the victims in their city's newspaper as a plea for others to lock their doors. A couple left their back door open to let the breezes in with just the screen door latched. A gang of four youths came in through the screen door. They robbed the husband, an ex-Marine, at gunpoint and tied him up. Then they raped his pregnant wife who was upstairs reading in bed when her assailants entered.

You not only need to use your locks, you need to ensure that all door locks and the door assemblies themselves will resist assault and cannot be jimmied open. This is as true for a door between an attached garage or basement and the home as it is for the main house entrances—front, back, and sides. In the event that an intruder gets into your garage or basement, you want to prevent further access to the house itself.

All entrance doors should be solid wood or metal overlay and at least 1-3/4 inches thick; hollow-core wooden doors are too easy to batter in or kick down. The door frame needs to be solidly constructed and the door should fit snugly in the frame; metal weather stripping can be added to fix the problem if it does not. The strike plate (the metal plate opposite the lock that the door bolt rests in) needs to be securely attached to the frame.

Check to see that the hinge pins on all entrance doors are on the inside of the doors. Otherwise, the pins can be removed and the door lifted out. If the hinge pins are on the outside of the door, replace the hinge pins with non-removable ones.

You need to be able to see who is outside your entrance doors without opening them. If your doors do not have peepholes, install wide-angle viewers that give you a 180-degree view or better (Figure 2), including the door to an attached garage. **A door chain provides no real protection and gives you a false sense of security**; it can be easily broken if an intruder throws his weight against the door. The trick is not to open the door in the first place.

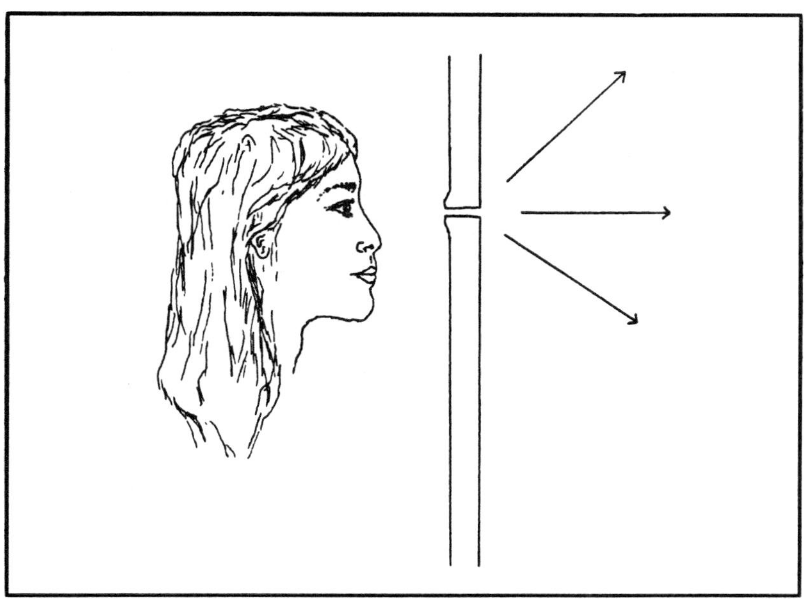

Figure 2. Wide-angle viewer for door

Door Locks

Many homes have spring-latch door locks. This type of lock can be easily opened with a plastic credit card or a knife blade inserted between the door and the door frame to push in the bolt. Replace them—now.

Instead use a sturdy, well-installed deadbolt lock made of case-hardened steel with a bolt that extends 1-1/2 inches into the door jamb. It should also come with a heavy-duty strike plate that is secured to the door jamb with 3-inch screws. If screws of this length cannot be used because of nearby sidelights to the door, then an extra long strike plate of 8-12 inches should be used instead.

The deadbolt lock can be keyed on the outside only (single cylinder) or on both sides (double cylinder). For the first, you lock or unlock the door from the inside with a turn knob. For the second, you must use a key whether entering or leaving the home.

The single-cylinder lock is preferable for any solid door without sidelights or windows close enough (within 40 inches of the lock) for a burglar to break the glass and reach in to turn the knob open. The double-cylinder lock is needed when there is glass in the door, sidelights, or close-by windows. Do not leave the key in the lock; a burglar could break the glass and let himself in. Keep the key in a near-by accessible place that all family members know about in case a quick exit is needed in an emergency, such as a fire.

If your local jurisdiction or building code restrictions preclude double-keyed locks, then you can install protective grilles over glass doors, sidelights, and nearby windows. For windows, be sure the grilles have a quick release mechanism so you can get out of the house in an emergency. Other options include replacing the panes with security glass or installing break-resistant polycarbonate over the windows on the inside. These materials are more expensive than regular glass panes, but they add protective value for your cost.

One woman was victimized twice by neighborhood youths who shot out her glass door with high-powered air rifles. The second attack occurred 2 days after the replacement glass was installed by her insurance company. This time she asked that bullet-proof plexiglass be installed. She was amazed to find that by paying a small additional amount she could buy the peace of mind that she would not return home again to find a shattered mess in her entranceway.

An additional way to help secure a solid entry door is a barricade lock that works on the same principle as tilting a chair under the doorknob. A barricade lock has a metal bar with one end braced against the middle of the door and the other end inserted at an angle into a holder bolted to the floor or wedged by friction against the floor (Figure 3).

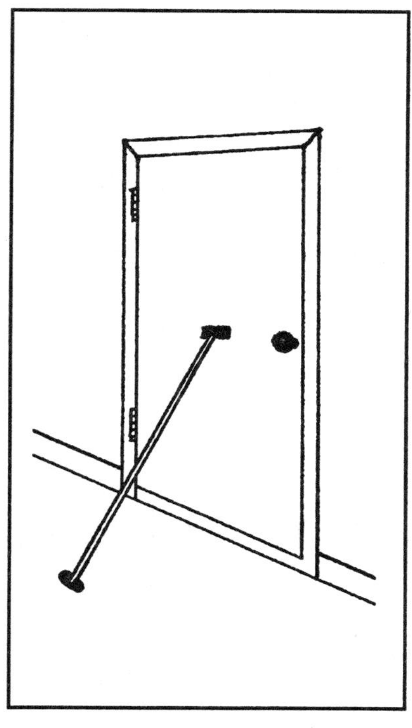

Figure 3. Barricade lock

Another method that is both quick and inexpensive is to reinforce your door from the inside by wedging two rubber doorstops against the base of the closed door. This technique is also portable, so you can pack a couple of doorstops in your suitcase whenever you travel.

Double doors (or French doors) are even more vulnerable to forced entry than single doors. The best type of auxiliary locks for these doors are 12-inch-long lever bolts of 1/2 inch diameter that are installed flush to the inside top and bottom edge of each door and slide into their respective holders when locked.

Sliding glass doors are always favorite targets. They more often than not are at the back of the house and not easily seen from the street. The locks can be defeated easily and the doors lifted out of their tracks. Once open, they allow a large exit area for removing bulky items from the house.

To reinforce sliding doors you need to prevent the door from being lifted and removed from the track. This can be done by installing large head metal screws along the upper track so that the door frame just clears the heads of the screws.

An **additional device** is needed to prevent the door from being slid open if the door lock is jimmied. Commercial anti-slide locks that can be installed on the lower track are available. A metal hinge bar or "Charlie bar" that goes across the middle of the inactive side as a brace against the sliding side can be purchased at any hardware or home improvement store. A thick wooden dowel or metal rod in the track of the closed door works well, too (Figure 4).

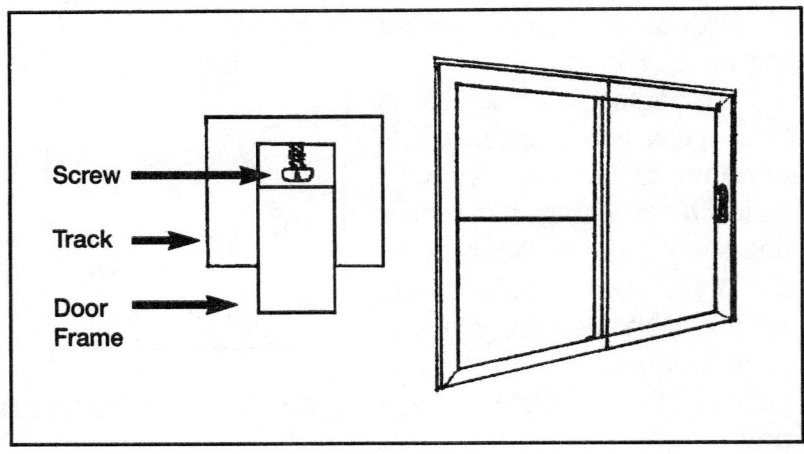

Figure 4. Metal screw in upper track and metal hinge bar

Window Security

For a burglar, a window that offers quick entry is just as good as a door. In some newer homes, floor to ceiling windows that let the light in are tall enough to permit easy access for a grown man. But the window does not have to be large to be inviting. A frequent favorite of burglars is a bathroom window because one is often found to be unlocked.

Windows should be kept locked at all times. If they are open for ventilation, they should still be locked in position, high enough for air to get in but not high enough for a person to squeeze through (a 3-inch clearance is a good rule). Depending on the type of window involved, there are a variety of commercial locking devices available, some that allow two positions—fully closed and partially opened for ventilation.

Window Locks

Most windows come with latches that provide little physical security even when closed. Besides it is easy enough for a burglar to cut out or break a pane of glass and reach in to undo the latch. So you need to add a backup lock or in some way bolster the physical security of the accessible windows in your home.

In high-crime areas or for especially vulnerable ground level or basement windows, lockable metal grilles, cross bars, or shutters make sense. Just be sure you get the kind that let you exit your home in an emergency and keep the key nearby but out of view in a location known by all family members.

The butterfly locks on double-hung windows are easily opened. Supplemental keyed locks are available at hardware and home improvement stores that can be installed on the sashes. Again, you will need to keep the keys readily accessible in case of an emergency.

Another method that works well to keep the window shut is to "pin" the two sashes together. You drill a hole sloping downward at an angle at each corner of the top rail of the inside window sash part way through the bottom rail of the outside window sash, and then insert a wide-head nail that is 1/4 inch longer than the hole you drilled into each hole. With the "pins" in place, the window can not be lifted from the outside. However, you can pull the "pins" out quickly from inside in case of emergency (Figure 5).

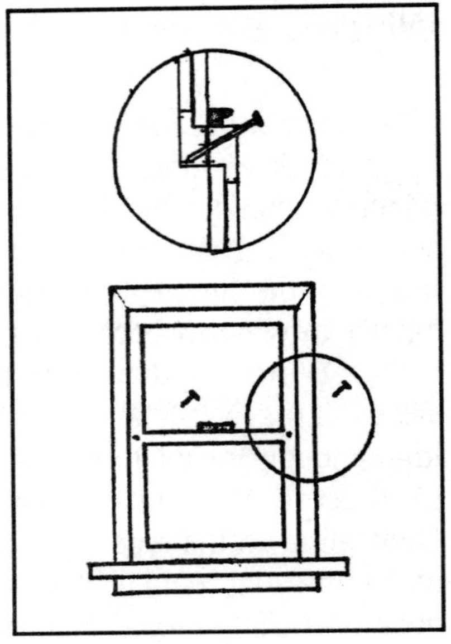

Figure 5. Pin window sashes

Sliding windows have the same problems as sliding glass doors and need to be fitted with anti-slide locks that can be purchased and installed. Some commercial locks screw into the track and can be adjusted to allow you to open the window slightly while preventing a person outside from opening it further. These windows also can be fitted with wooden dowels or metal rods in the inside lower track to prevent opening plus screws across the top track to prevent lifting as previously explained for sliding glass doors in the section on door locks.

Casement windows need to be checked to ensure the operator handle or crank does not have excessive play and cannot be worked loose. Keyed locks are available to reinforce this type of window.

Louvre windows are the least secure of all because the glass panes can easily be removed. These should either be replaced with a more secure type of window or protected with metal screening or grating on the inside. If you have an enclosed porch with jalousie windows, valuables left on the porch are not well protected. Also, be sure that the door and windows leading to the house from the porch are secure.

Window Air Conditioners

The most secure installation for a room-size air conditioning unit is in the wall. If the unit is placed in an open window, then it needs to be securely mounted and reinforced in some way to prevent a burglar from removing the unit and gaining entry through that window. Secure the unit to the window frame with metal brackets and long screws or attach a metal brace across the unit that is bolted to the 2x4 wall stud on either side of the window. Also lock the window in place so it can't be lifted any higher than the opening for the air conditioning unit.

Attached Garages

Attached garages can be a great point of entry to your home while providing concealment for the burglar. Keep your garage doors locked, even when you are just working in the yard. If there are windows in the garage, these need extra locks the same as those to the house. Garage doors with automatic openers can be forced open, and frequencies for the electronic openers may be duplicated with little effort. Either an additional lock for the garage door or a security device for your opener is needed.

You can secure a standard overhead garage door on tracks by installing a case-hardened padlock through a hole in the track above the roller. With garage doors that open out rather than rolling up on a track, install a padlock on the doors, and if the hinges are on the outside, replace the hinge pins with a non-removable type.

If the attic of your house is accessible through a crawl space from the attic of the garage, you need to secure the opening to the garage attic with a case-hardened padlock and hasp with the screws hidden when the hasp is closed.

Your Home Interior

Assuming you have taken the necessary precautions to secure your yard and your home, you still need to consider the possibility that a burglar can gain entrance to your home. In the event that this happens, there are three prime concerns:

- You need an early warning system to alert others and yourself.
- You need to create a safe haven within your home that can give you extra protection, buy you time, and provide a way to get help or escape.
- You need to hide valuables and make it less likely that the burglar will take them with him.

Security Systems

Studies show that having an alarm system greatly reduces your chances of being burglarized, even more so if you have the kind of system that is hooked into a central monitoring facility that can respond by dispatching police, fire, or emergency medic personnel. Insurance companies recognize this fact in the premiums they charge for homeowner's insurance. Many offer discounts based on the security measures you put in place, such as deadbolt locks and an alarm system.

A home alarm system today can cost anything from a few hundred dollars to several thousand, depending on the sophistication, features, and coverage that the system affords. You need to do some research and make comparisons to determine the system that is right for your situation and fits your pocketbook.

A security system decal alone can be a deterrent to the casual thief; whether or not you actually have an alarm. These can be purchased from Radio Shack and other stores and should be placed on doors and accessible windows. However, a seasoned burglar may look for other signs that an actual system is installed.

There is a vast array of security devices and systems to choose from, some protecting individual entry points or areas in the home, others that cover a whole house. There are both hard-wired and wireless systems that operate on the same principle as your TV's remote control. All alarm system wiring should be in the house to prevent a burglar from cutting it. Some perimeter alarms go off when a contact is broken on a door or window. Other systems have sensors that detect motion or body heat. The more expensive systems include surveillance cameras.

Your local hardware or home improvement store can give you information on the types of off-the-shelf systems available, but any do-it-yourself system that offers an effective deterrent to the would-be intruder will take some electronic know-how for proper installation.

If you have someone else install a system or you use a residential alarm company, make sure the individual or business is reputable and employees are bonded and insured. Ask for written estimates of the work and a copy of the contract you'll be signing. Be sure you understand all the costs involved for the equipment, installation, and monthly service fee, if any. Do some comparison shopping before you decide.

You can call the National Burglar and Fire Alarm Association at 301-907-3202 for a list of member companies in your area. Any company you consider should be licensed and certified by Underwriters Laboratories. Call your local Better Business Bureau to ensure there are no complaints registered against a company. Insist on referrals from customers that you can contact to verify the quality of the work performed and their satisfaction with the services provided. Call these referrals. You may be surprised at what they tell you.

Good alarm systems have emergency backup power from batteries so that a power outage or a burglar that cuts the power source will not put the system out of action. Devices that turn the system on and off should be tamper-proof. Keep your alarm system on at night, when you are away, and when you are at home during the day. Your system may have different settings to cover these uses with various delays before activation. Be sure you and everyone in your home knows the proper way to operate the system and **use it**.

A portable remote panic button gives you mobility and allows you to manually activate the alarm at the first sign of trouble. It can serve to scare off a burglar before completing a break-in of your home or be used as a distress signal in other situations as well.

False alarms can be a problem, and the potential for such should be a major consideration in determining the security system that is right for your needs. Some police departments fine the owner for responding to a false alarm. Any system you choose should have a timer that shuts the alarm off after a maximum of 10 minutes; an unattended alarm can be a major disturbance to neighbors.

Furry Friends

If you like pets and are willing to take on the responsibility, a dog can discourage burglars as well as provide company. A good watchdog will alert you to any noise and is sensitive to strange scents. Because dogs are territorial by nature, they will bark or howl at intruders. Criminals know this and it gives them pause. In several studies of prison inmates, dogs were identified as the best alarm systems available. Larger dogs are viewed as the greater threat, but even smaller dogs can be a noisy deterrent.

In choosing a dog, you need to consider the size of your home, your lifestyle, and your willingness to provide the care and attention needed. The best pet is one that has undergone obedience training; it will help the animal be a better protector. As a pet owner, you are liable for the actions of your dog so you do not want the animal attacking friends, family members, or innocent people by mistake.

To be most effective, the dog needs free range in either your fenced yard or the interior of your home. A dog that is chained to a post or locked in one room of the house will not be viewed as a serious threat. However, a dog racing from one window to another and barking frantically will probably send a would-be intruder to another house where there is no pet. Be sure to post "Beware of Dog" signs prominently if you have a dog—and even if you do not. Those signs alone might convince a burglar to go elsewhere.

Safe Room

Fortify at least one room inside your home that you and your family can retreat to in the event of a break-in and summon help. In most cases, this will be the master bedroom. If you live alone, this bedroom "fortress" becomes especially important for added security when you are asleep at night.

The safe room should have a solid core door and deadbolt lock, a rechargeable flashlight plugged into an electrical outlet, and a cellular phone. Otherwise, a burglar can cut your phone wires or simply lift an extension phone off the hook to make the other extensions useless for calling out.

If you are single, lock the door when you retire for the night. If there are other family members, be sure they know to gather in this room for protection at the first sign of trouble. If the bedroom is on the second floor, you can buy a roll-out fire ladder that can be used to escape in case of fire or to evacuate your family if your home is invaded. Be sure to practice using the ladder with all family members.

Protecting Valuables

The best way to protect small but expensive items, such as jewelry and coins, from being taken from your house is to keep them in a bank safe deposit box. Large sums of cash should not be kept in the home, either. For the rest of your valuables, you have two ways to reduce the chance they will be taken—one is to hide them and the other is to mark them.

If you have a home safe, make it the kind that is permanently installed in a wall or bolted to the floor and hide it from view. Place a piece of furniture in front of the wall opening or put the safe behind a false wall under the basement stairwell or in a closet.

Most burglars know people like to keep valuables in the master bedroom, so do not do this. Better to locate hiding places in the kitchen cupboard or behind library shelves in the family room, than to keep items in the first place a burglar will look.

If you get creative about hiding places, such as inside detergent containers or above drop ceiling tiles, make a note of where you put things or you may forget your secret hiding spots. One woman tossed out an old box from her closet when she moved, forgetting that she had hidden a $3,000 ring in it.

Property that cannot be hidden should be marked with an identifying number (for example, your driver's license number and state abbreviation); it is less likely to be taken. This is especially true for TVs, VCRs, music systems, computers, and cameras. You can use an engraving tool to etch the number in electronic items or an ultraviolet pen to mark the back of other types of valuables such as oriental rugs or paintings.

Check with your local police department and library to see if they offer an "Operation I.D." program where they will loan you tools and provide decals to place in your windows to warn off burglars that your valuables are marked. Criminals know this makes it difficult to sell the items and easier to be prosecuted if they are caught with stolen property in their possession. Police can also return items to their rightful owners when they are recovered.

You should also make a complete inventory of your property, listing items room by room, including serial numbers of those items that have them, and approximate costs. Supplement the list with either still photographs or a video of your possessions and include sales receipts and appraisals to verify the value and replacement costs if items are stolen. Keep this inventory file in a bank safe deposit box or other secure place.

Apartment Security

The same advice for homeowners on landscaping and lighting, key control, installing and using secondary locks for doors and windows, wide-angle peepholes, alarm systems, a safe room, and protecting valuables also applies to people living in apartments, condominiums, and co-ops. If these added security measures are not provided by management, it is worth the cost to reinforce the unit you live in. You have no way of controlling who has access to the master key, and this puts you at greater risk.

When choosing a complex, call the local police department first and ask about the past crime history of the area and the complex. Visit the complex at night and look the area over from a safety standpoint for lighting, groups congregating, and other factors. Get specifics from the management office on any security measures taken by the complex—coverage by guards or security patrols, whether locks are changed for new tenants, if tenants are notified when crimes are committed within the complex.

Record what you are told and by whom and any other safety issues that are raised while you are a tenant—this is important for holding the owner liable if you become a victim of crime. You should also put all your requests for improved security measures, such as replacing locks or the need for additional lighting, in writing for the same reason.

The National Crime Prevention Council offers a safety checklist for evaluating your apartment building:

- Is there some kind of control over who enters and leaves the building?
- Are walkways, entrances, parking areas, elevators, hallways, stairways, laundry rooms, and storage areas well-lighted, 24 hours a day?
- Are fire stairs locked from the stairwell side?
- Are mailboxes in a well-traveled, well-lighted area and do they have good locks?
- Is management good about safety issues—trimming shrubs, replacing burnt-out lights promptly, removing trash and snow?

If you are single, it is better not to take a ground floor apartment because there is more risk of break-in. If you must be in a basement or ground floor unit, ensure that well-secured grilles or grates that can be opened from the inside are installed over the windows and other extra safety measures are taken.

Maintenance people should not show up at your apartment unannounced or enter without your permission, especially when you are at home. Tell the management office that you want a written notice each time your unit is entered, stating who entered your apartment, the date and time, and what work was performed. If someone from maintenance comes to your door unexpectedly, call the management office to confirm the person was sent for a legitimate purpose.

Campus Residences

Many campus crimes happen within student residence halls and dormitories, so additional security measures need to be taken when you move in. Have the locks rekeyed; add supplemental locks to the door and windows, and **keep them locked at all times**. Portable alarms for doors and windows are available at reasonable cost as an extra safety precaution. If the door does not have a wide-angle viewer, install one. You should also mark your valuables and register them with campus security.

If you have roommates, it is critical to set up safety rules with each other from the beginning and openly discuss any behavior that puts others at risk. One freshman awoke at midnight to find a strange man climbing into bed with her, the drunken friend of her roommate's date that had walked in with the couple. The roommate seemed unconcerned about the threat to the other woman's safety. The freshman reported the incident to campus security and demanded a room change and a more responsible roommate.

You also need to check the general security of the building the same way an apartment dweller would assess a complex:

- Is there any control on who gains entrance to the building? Are outer doors locked in the evening or security monitored in some other way, such as closed-circuit television cameras?
- Are all stairways, hallways, other common areas, such as vending machine or laundry rooms, and the outside of the building well-lighted?
- What help can campus security offer to increase your safety? Are there patrols? If so, where and when?
- Who do you call to report suspicious situations to or to enlist help if someone tries to get into your room?

Key Points To Remember

- Always lock all doors and windows of your home.
- Make the home look occupied and well-tended.
- Provide several levels of security to make break-ins difficult.
- Conduct a security audit of your home and correct deficiencies.
- Secure valuables in your yard and store items in locked buildings.
- Keep landscaping in check and provide good outside lighting.
- Safeguard keys, and rekey locks when keys are lost or stolen.
- Install sturdy deadbolt locks on all entrance doors.
- Use additional locking devices on sliding glass doors and windows.
- Reinforce security for attached garages and attic access.
- Install a security alarm system and/or get a watchdog.
- Fortify one room in your home to provide safety from intruders.
- Inventory and mark your possessions.
- Evaluate apartments and campus residences for security measures.

Practice Scenarios

What if...?

You go to put the cat out one morning and notice that your back door to the screened porch is unlocked and the screen door is not latched.

Your teenage son comes home and tells you that his key chain has "mysteriously disappeared."

You come back from a quick trip to the supermarket and remember you left the family room window partially open to let in the breeze.

You hear noises outside your home at night, and when you pick up the phone, the line is dead.

You return from a friend's party at night and notice that the light on the landing of your apartment unit is out.

Home Security Audit Checklist

Evaluate the security of your home according to the items listed:

Home Exterior

- ☐ Is your yard well-maintained?
- ☐ Do gates and outbuildings have secure locks?
- ☐ Are items such as bikes, tools, ladders, and lawn equipment out of sight and under lock?
- ☐ Are shrubs and trees around your home cut back to eliminate cover for intruders?
- ☐ Do you have thorny bushes planted as natural barriers under ground floor windows?
- ☐ Do exterior lights illuminate all entrances and the perimeter of your home?
- ☐ Are outside power and fuse boxes securely locked?
- ☐ Is your street address number clearly displayed on your mailbox and house?

Doors and Windows

- ☐ Are all entrance doors solid core wood or metal?
- ☐ Are the door frames and strike plates strong and secure?
- ☐ Are door hinge pins on the inside or the non-removable type?
- ☐ Do all exterior doors have wide-angle peepholes?
- ☐ Does each entrance door have a deadbolt lock with a 1-1/2 inch bolt, including the basement and garage doors?
- ☐ Are door panels and side lights made of security glass or break-resistant plastic or protected by grilles?
- ☐ Do double doors (French doors) have additional lever bolt locks on both doors?
- ☐ Are sliding glass doors reinforced with locks or rods to prevent jimmying or lifting the doors from the track?
- ☐ Do accessible windows have additional locks or pins to prevent opening or are they protected by grilles?
- ☐ Are window air conditioners securely locked in place?
- ☐ Are garage doors and attic openings reinforced with padlocks?

Key Control

- ☐ Do you keep a spare key with a trusted neighbor?
- ☐ Are extra keys in your home in a secure place and out of sight?
- ☐ Do you keep house keys separate from car keys and never leave them with parking attendants or car service places?
- ☐ Do you rekey locks whenever you move into a new home or a key is lost or stolen?

Other Measures

- ☐ Do you have an alarm system?
- ☐ Do you own a dog?
- ☐ Have you set up a "safe room" with solid door and deadbolt lock, flashlight, and cellular phone?
- ☐ Are valuables locked up and hidden away?
- ☐ Is your property marked with an identifying number?
- ☐ Do you have a master inventory of your possessions?

7

Safely Home Alone

Thelma heard the doorbell ring. She went to the entrance and looked through the peephole. A nicely dressed young man stood there. She did not know him, so she said through the door, "What do you want, please?" He said, "Hello, my name is Tom. We are selling $1 raffle tickets to raise money for computers in our school. Will you help us by buying a ticket?" That seemed harmless enough. She unlocked the door and as she began to open it, "Tom" pushed his way in. He pulled out a knife and said, "Don't make a sound." He marched her up the stairs and tied her hands tightly to the bedposts. Then he emptied her jewelry box contents into the knapsack he was carrying and took the cash from her wallet. She was still tied and trembling when her husband came home from work 2 hours later, stunned by what had happened and realizing that it could have been much worse.

Screening Strangers

The strongest doors and the best locks mean nothing if you willingly open your door to strangers. If you have installed wide-angle viewers on all exterior doors, then you should not have to open your door to see who is on the other side. Many burglaries, rapes, and murders have occurred because women were not good gatekeepers of their own security.

Never open your door to people you do not know. First verify who they say they are and then determine that they have a legitimate reason to be entering your home. Even then, you should be on guard for your personal safety and the protection of your valuables. Do not leave yourself vulnerable to attack by workmen or provide temptation by leaving your purse or other valuables out where they can be seen.

If you are expecting someone to provide a home service or repair, ask the workman to hold up his identity card and then phone the business office to verify the name as an employee. When someone shows up at your door unexpected, ask for a photo I.D., and then call the organization that the person represents and check out him and his story, before allowing him in your home.

Do not let a uniform fool you, not even that of a police officer. Many criminals use a uniform as a way to reduce suspicion. Be sure to look up the number yourself of the company, utility, or precinct or get it from directory assistance. If you use a number conveniently provided by the person, he might have an accomplice standing by to answer that phone.

When people come knocking at your door, trying to sell you a service, a product, or a political or religious cause, tell them firmly and politely that you do not accept unsolicited calls under any circumstances. You can advise them to leave any information they have outside your door, and that you will get back with them for an appointment if you are interested.

Be especially cautious of "home improvement" companies that happen to be in your area and offer a "special discount." Do not let a representative into your home on any pretext. Get written estimates of any work being proposed, and check out the company. Many burglary rings use this approach to case neighborhoods and gain access to homes.

Remember, anyone can print up a business card, so be sure to check out the legitimacy and reputation of a company before doing business. One successful burglary ring offered cut-rate moving services. Unfortunately for the people that went for this "bargain," the moving van never showed up at the intended destination. The stolen property was stashed at a warehouse until it could be fenced.

Even when you are expecting a delivery, ask for identification before opening your door and signing for the package or item. In the movie "Death Wish," a middle-aged woman and her grown daughter leave a grocery order to be delivered to the mother's apartment. Some punks in the store see the address and show up ahead of the delivery, but say they have the grocery order. They gain entry to the apartment, and when their robbery of the two women yields little cash, they kick the mother to death and rape the daughter.

If the delivery is unexpected, ask for a photo I.D. and verify with the home office first, before opening your door. Otherwise, you can ask that the item be left outside; if a signature slip is needed for receipt, ask that it be slid under your door. You can also refuse delivery at that time or ask where you can pick it up. Fake deliveries are a favorite ploy of many criminals.

If someone comes banging on your door with an "emergency," offer to make the necessary phone calls for help, but **do not open your door**. One criminal claimed he was being attacked to gain entry into homes. Others say the car has broken down, there's been a serious accident, or someone is having a heart attack.

You do not want to refuse help in case it is genuinely needed, just do it from your side of the door. Call 911 and get the people who are trained to deal with real emergencies. Call road service or the person's family, if asked. If your offer to make the call is turned down or the person disappears, call the police and report it immediately. Someone else in your neighborhood might fall prey to the same ruse.

Every time you open the door to someone you do not know, you are at risk. So do not be embarrassed to protect your safety and the safety of your family by not opening the door. When you do open the door, be wary and pay attention. If you have a burglar alarm with a portable panic button remote control, have it in your hand when you answer the door.

You might think it would be a better idea not to answer the door at all, but this would be a mistake. If nobody comes to the door, a burglar may decide the house or apartment is empty and therefore a good target for break-in.

Never admit you are home alone. Call out, "I'll get the door," as you approach it so it seems as if there is someone else with you. If a man is asked for, say, "He's indisposed at the moment," or "I can't disturb him right now." If the caller is persistent, tell him your husband is in the shower and the caller will have to wait a few minutes for him to come out, then call the police.

If you live in an apartment complex with a buzzer system for entry, never buzz in someone you do not know. Also, do not let strangers go in with you when you open the main door. It is up to the person being visited to let a caller in. Report to management any other occupants who routinely let strangers in. Once a person is given access to a building, all occupants are at risk. Several women have been raped and murdered because someone else in their buildings let a stranger in on some pretext.

If someone says he is an occupant of the building but forgot his keys, is visiting his sister, has a delivery for a neighbor, or needs to do some repairs, tell him you cannot buzz him in but you will alert the building manager or superintendent to come to the door. If he replies, "You do not need to contact the manager," call the police and report the situation. Under no circumstances should you let the person in. There have been many cases where a criminal simply buzzed one apartment after another until someone let him in.

Some criminals scan mailboxes or telephone directories looking for single women as targets. Women used to be advised to use their first initial only with their last names on their mailboxes and for their telephone listings, but this advice is so well known among criminals that it no longer works and might even call attention to your single status. You need to make it appear that you are not alone. Use the last name only in plural—The Smiths—or Mr. and Mrs. Smith, so it seems like a family or a couple lives there rather than an individual.

Since it is easy to steal from a mailbox, it also makes sense to have your paycheck or any other regular payment you receive handled through an electronic funds transfer for direct deposit into a bank account rather than sending a check to your home.

As for your telephone listing, the best bet for a single woman is to have an unlisted phone number—it will greatly reduce your chances of unwanted attention.

Telephone Tactics

Be sure to post emergency and other key numbers by each phone; in a real emergency you will not have time to look these up. You should also keep a pad of paper and a pencil by each phone in case you are called about an emergency or you call someone at your home when you are out and important details need to be noted. A wonderful screener for phone calls is a telephone answering machine or a voice mail service through your phone company. Either will discourage annoying calls. Each prevents the phone from "ringing off the wall" when you are out or on vacation. Often burglars will call a residence first to see if anyone is home to answer the phone.

If you are married, have your husband record the message. If you are single, ask a male friend or relative to make the recording. Do not give your name or specifics. Keep the message vague. For example, "We are not available to answer the phone at the moment, but please leave a message and we will get back to you as soon as we can."

Many criminals consider the telephone a tool of the trade. They use it to get the information they need—sometimes to set up a burglary, sometimes to con you in other ways—for instance, to get credit card numbers so they can use your accounts or to get money from you for phony investments. A caller may tell you that you have won a prize, he is taking a survey, or he is an employee of your bank. **Do not give out personal or financial information to strangers over the phone.**

Also, telefraud is an equal opportunity employer—this is one area where women con artists may be used to gain your trust. In the same way that you should refuse unsolicited calls at your door, be firm but polite about not accepting phone offers. Tell callers to send you information by mail and you will get back to them if interested. If they persist, or tell you it's a "now or never deal," hang up.

If a survey request seems legitimate, make an appointment to answer questions at a later date. Get a company or agency name, address, and representative's name. Then check out the organization and the survey being conducted before responding.

Never give out your marital status over the phone, and **never admit to being home alone.** If someone asks to speak to the "man of the house," say "I can't disturb him now," and ask to take a message. Do not say, "He's at work," or "He's on a business trip," or "I'm divorced."

Also, do not give out your schedule over the phone. When you are trying to set up an appointment for any reason, never discuss the rest of your calendar. Just say, "I could make it on Thursday at 10 a.m." or "That wouldn't be possible," if you need a different date or time. No one knows just how trustworthy the people you talk to are or whether they will pass the information on to someone with criminal intent.

Beware of "wrong number" calls as well and do not give out any information, not your name or phone number. Just ask, "What number did you dial?" If it is not your number, simply say, "Then you have the wrong number." If it is your number, ask, "Who were you trying to reach?" If there is no one by that name in your household, say "We don't have anyone here by that name." If you get repeated "wrong numbers," report it to your telephone company.

If you receive obscene or threatening calls, hang up as soon as you realize what is happening. Do not say anything. You do not want the caller to get an emotional reaction from you. The obscene caller has two purposes—to get away with unacceptable behavior and to exercise power over another—from the safety that the anonymous phone call allows him and with little chance that he will be caught. You do not have to indulge his fantasies or give him the satisfaction of upsetting you.

Often these calls are random, although it might be someone you know. But if you get repeat calls, notify your telephone company and the police of the dates, times, and content, and describe the caller's voice as best you can. These calls are usually more annoying than dangerous, but if a caller tells you he is following you or intends to do you bodily harm, get the police involved immediately—you may have a stalker on your hands.

Consider getting "caller I.D." or a similar device that records the phone number of the person calling you. The information it gives you can be invaluable to the phone company and police in following up on your complaint.

Home at Night

If you follow the precautions on handling strangers at the door and on the phone, you will go a long way toward ensuring your personal safety when you are by yourself at night. **Be sure that blinds and shades are completely closed** so your whereabouts cannot be monitored from the street. It is easy for someone outside to see you in lighted rooms when it is dark out. Go outside and view your house; you might be surprised to see how visible the interior of your home is at night.

It is also a good idea to keep lights on in more than one room or keep a radio or TV on in a room you are not in. That makes your home seem occupied by more than one person.

Make sure all the doors and windows are locked. If you have an alarm system with a panic button, keep it with you at all times. If you see anything suspicious or you think someone is trying to break in, do not go investigating. Call the police immediately.

Returning Home

If you go shopping and come home with groceries or packages, bring them all to your door before you unlock it. If you unlock the door first and then bring your bags or items in one at a time, there is a chance that someone can slip into your home between your trips to the car.

Whenever you go out for the evening, be sure to leave some lights on in different rooms and a TV or radio playing. Even if someone is casing your home and sees you leave, he will think there are others remaining in the house. Never leave a note on your door saying you are out and when you expect to return.

When you return, have your key ready so you do not delay in entering your home. If you enter through an attached garage with an automatic opener, first check that nothing seems disturbed. Then, with the garage lights on and the garage door down, you can promptly enter your house and close and lock the door.

If something does not look right, you see a door or window open, broken glass, lights out, or any other sign that someone has broken in, **do not enter the house**. You do not want to surprise a burglar or prevent his escape—he could be armed and become violent. Go to a neighbor or use a pay or cellular phone and call the police. Report a "burglary in progress" to get a quick response.

If all family members are going to be out of the house at the same time for a publicized event, such as a wedding or a funeral, see if you can get someone to housesit while you are gone, or at least ask a neighbor to keep an extra lookout. There are burglars that comb the newspapers, looking for this type of "opportunity" to hit an unoccupied home.

Home Intruders

The only thing more upsetting than to find your home has been burglarized is for it to happen while you are there. If you have a choice, **never** confront the burglars. If you can, get out quickly and quietly and call the police from a neighbor's place. Or go to the "safe room," lock yourself in, and call from there.

Be sure the police dispatcher knows the crime is happening now and that you are at risk. Provide as much information as possible; it is best to stay on the phone. But lay low, waiting for help to arrive. Choose an area of the room with cover and protection for yourself and family members. Burglars will generally leave without contact unless challenged.

If you are awakened in bed by an intruder in your room, experts advise that you pretend to be asleep until he leaves. You would be at a disadvantage under the best of circumstances since you cannot see in the dark and you do not know if he is armed. But stay alert and be prepared to react in case you are physically accosted.

Should you accidentally surprise a burglar face-to-face, stay calm and be cooperative. If threatened, he may react violently, especially if he is on drugs. Your possessions are not worth risking your life. If you are going to defend yourself from bodily harm, that is a different situation, but do not jump in to defend your property. Try to be observant, though, so you can give a good description to the police later.

Extended Trips

Vacations and business trips will require the help of a neighbor and some planning ahead so that your home looks occupied while you are gone. Let only a trusted few know you will be gone and do not discuss your plans in public. Never announce your trip in the newspaper before you leave.

You need to arrange for the upkeep of your yard while you are gone, with the grass mowed or snow removed, depending on the season. You could stop deliveries of mail and newspapers, but then you are going public about your absence. Better to have a neighbor collect these and any circulars left at your door for you daily.

It also helps to put some trash out for collection, because empty trash cans can be another sign that no one is at home. A car parked in your driveway gives the impression that someone is home. See if one of your neighbors will put some trash out in front of your house or park a car in your driveway. Or you can leave your own car in the driveway if you do not need it for the trip; just be sure that both the car and the garage are locked.

If you can enlist the help of a neighbor to open and close blinds and shades each day, that is preferable to leaving them in the same position. If not, it is better to leave them partially opened. A closed up house announces the occupants are gone. You also need to use timers throughout your home to turn on lights and a radio or TV at different times during the evening as if people were at home.

If you hire a housesitter, make sure the person is reliable and responsible. Check out any petsitting service as well to ensure the company is reputable. Whether you pay someone, or your neighbor, a relative, or a friend is willing to help out as a favor, be sure to discuss the security measures of your home and get a commitment that the person will be conscientious about locking up and activating the alarm system.

You can also alert your local police station when you are going to be gone and ask that a police patrol check on your home periodically.

Repeat Burglaries

It is an unfortunate fact, but true: once your home has been burglarized, it is more likely to be burglarized again. If the burglars found your home to be an easy target, why not come back again? These intruders now know what kind of valuables you have. They may come to get what they left behind the first time. Or they could wait until your insurance claim is settled and you have replaced the items.

In one case, a burglar gained entrance to a home twice in one month through the same unlocked window. In another case, the apartment of a young bank vice-president in New York was hit three times in as many weeks—the last time they took the sheets off her bed. In yet another case, two men were so taken by photos of a teenage daughter they saw while burglarizing an unoccupied home that they returned when the family was there. They abducted the girl through her bedroom window and sexually molested her before she was able to escape from them.

You must take immediate action to prevent a repeat performance. Correct whatever weaknesses there were in your security measures that allowed the first break-in. Step up precautions and be on the alert. Do not think that because it has already "happened" to you, you are somehow protected from it happening again. You should get your locks rekeyed if there is any chance that the intruders had access to a spare key.

Neighbors Can Help

Get to know your neighbors, and be a good neighbor yourself. Decent people looking out for each other can provide the best defense against crime where you live. Join or start a Neighborhood Watch group. Work with your local police or sheriff's department—it can usually serve as a sponsor and provide guidance and information materials.

A Neighborhood Watch program can reinforce the basics of home security—precautions that individuals should take as well as ways of helping each other. It also means that neighbors are watching out for suspicious activities and reporting them to the police. Posted signs that your area is protected by a Neighborhood Watch program may warn burglars off.

Key Points To Remember

- Never open your door to strangers or anyone that does not have an appointment.
- Always verify the identity of visitors, even if they are expected.
- If a stranger knocks on your door and asks to use the phone for an emergency, offer to make the call, but do not open your door.
- Never admit that you are home alone to visitors or callers.
- Never allow a stranger access to a group residence building.
- If you are single, do not put your name alone on a mailbox, and get an unlisted phone number.
- Never give out personal or financial information to strangers over the phone.

- If you receive obscene or threatening phone calls, hang up immediately.
- Always keep blinds, shades, and curtains drawn closed at night.
- If your home looks disturbed, do not enter it; a break-in may be in progress.
- If you hear an intruder, escape from your house or go to your safe room, and call the police.
- If an intruder comes into your bedroom, pretend to be asleep.
- When you go on a trip, arrange for someone to watch your house and make it look lived in; also notify the police you will be away.
- If your house is burglarized, take immediate action to improve security to prevent it from happening again.
- Join or start a Neighborhood Watch program to improve the overall security of where you live.

Practice Scenarios

What if...?

Your doorbell rings and the man you see outside your peephole is wearing a uniform and carrying a box.

The caller says that he is an examiner at the bank and needs to go over some account information with you by phone.

You park your car in the garage and notice that the door into the house is off the hinges.

You are carrying your groceries to your back door and, as you put the key in the lock and turn the door knob, someone suddenly pushes you inside.

You awake in the middle of the night and hear someone moving around the foot of your bed.

You notice a young man in a jogging suit walking around to the basement windows of your neighbor's house.

8

Travel Tips

Allison was in the city attending a regional teachers' conference. Tired from a day of meetings, she had ordered a room service dinner and placed the tray outside her door when finished. She was just settling on the bed to watch some TV when there was a knock on the door. The man said he was from hotel security and he had to check the water sprinkling system in her room which was malfunctioning. When she opened the door, he smiled, and said he would only be a minute. As she backed into the room, he shut the door and flashed the knife he had taken from her tray outside the door. Allison was stunned as the man ordered her to the bed. He tied her hands behind her back, gagged her with a handkerchief, and raped her. Then he opened Allison's purse on the bedside table and took her money before leaving her bound on the hotel bed.

Hotel and Motel Security

Women are victims when they travel more often than you might think. That is why you need to plan trips for safety and be careful in hotels. Many people have a false sense of security when staying in commercial lodgings. Hotels and motels can provide you sleeping accommodations, but they are anything but safe.

Of course, the hospitality industry does not want you to know this—it is bad for business. Law suits against facilities for crimes committed because security was lax are kept quiet. Frequently, cases are settled out of court or court records are sealed. You are in double jeopardy from both fire and crime when you stay in commercial lodgings, so some extra precautions are needed.

The biggest problem with commercial lodgings is key control. Not only does the manager have master keys, but so do other employees. Also, former employees or previous guests may have made copies of keys or still have "lost" keys in their possession. Unfortunately, many places do not rekey rooms when this happens. If possible, pick hotels with electronic key systems that rekey each room after each guest checks out. You can call ahead to find out if the hotel does this.

Try to stay in reputable establishments, although security measures may not be sufficient even in expensive hotels. Use a travel agency you trust or an auto club to get recommendations on lodgings in safe areas rather than marginal areas where crime rates are higher. It is better to book your room ahead than to take chances on what lodgings will be available when you arrive. Get a guaranteed reservation if you will arrive after dark.

If you arrive at a hotel by car, use valet parking if it is available, and let the bellhops help you with your luggage. That way you will not be walking unfamiliar streets each time you park the car, and you will not be lugging suitcases which would put you at a disadvantage for protecting yourself against street crime. Otherwise, select a nearby secure parking garage recommended by the hotel management. If you are forced to park on the street overnight, choose a well-lit area.

Upon arrival, ask the front desk if someone is on duty 24 hours a day. If not, you need to know what hours coverage is provided. Find out both the number to call hotel management and the number to call local police in an emergency or if you feel threatened in any way.

When checking in, do not let a front desk clerk compromise your safety or privacy by loudly announcing your name or room number so that others nearby may hear this information. If this happens, ask to be assigned to another room.

Try to arrange for a room assignment on the second to sixth floors. These are your safest choices when staying at a hotel. Because these floors are above ground level, it is unlikely that your room will be broken into from the outside, but they are still low enough for firefighting and rescue equipment to reach.

If there is a fire escape outside your room when you check in, ask to be moved to another room, especially if you are a woman traveling alone. It is too easy for street criminals to gain access to your room this way.

Have someone on the hotel staff accompany you to your room and make sure everything is in order, and the phone is connected, before you accept your accommodations. Have this person show you how the locks work on the door and windows and how to operate lights and room climate control.

Do a security check on your room immediately—while the hotel staff is there. The door should have a peephole, a deadbolt lock, and an additional safety lock that operates from inside the room. Always use both locks when you are in the room. If the room has a connecting door, make sure it is locked.

Check that all windows and any sliding glass doors are closed and locked; sliding doors should have a secondary locking device for added security. Look inside the closets to be sure that someone is not hiding there. You should do a quick security check on your room each time you subsequently return to it as well.

Once you check into a room, read the fire safety instructions. Locate the nearest emergency exit to your room and count the number of doors to it—you might have to feel your way out through a smoke-filled hallway in the event of fire. You need to mentally plan your exit route in case it should become necessary.

Note where the ventilation grille is. If you were trapped in your room by fire outside your door, you could cover it with a wet towel to prevent smoke from being drawn into your room. Also check to see how the windows operate and if there is a ledge outside; consider whether you could escape that way if you had no other choice.

Find out where the vending and ice machines are located, but it is not a good idea to go to these areas alone, especially at night. In fact, if you are a woman traveling alone, and room service is available to you, it is worth the extra cost in added security to have these items brought to you.

If you order room service, be sure to look out the peephole when someone knocks at your door to verify it is your order. When you are done, call to have the tray picked up. Again verify that it is hotel staff before opening your door, or leave the tray outside your door for pickup once you have called.

Where maid service is concerned, do not put the "Please Clean My Room" sign on the door; this just announces that your room is unoccupied. Call housekeeping direct and ask that your room be cleaned after a certain time when you know you will be out of the room.

Never leave money, jewelry, or travel tickets in your hotel room while you are out. Use the hotel safe for all valuables, and be sure to get a receipt. Room door locks are notoriously easy to defeat. Even if they are not, just too many people can gain access to your room. It is not unusual for busy hotel staffs to mistakenly give out extra keys to new guests for rooms that are already occupied.

For extra security when you are in the room, use a travel lock that you can purchase to secure your room door or wedge rubber doorstops against the room door from inside. Never admit anyone to your room without positive identification. If someone knocks on your door or calls your room, ask for a name and get specifics on why they want to enter your room. Then call the front office and speak to a manager to verify the information you have been given.

Motels present some special problems because the rooms are more accessible and there is usually less security than in the more controlled environment of a hotel. Always park as close to your room as possible, and try to arrive during daylight.

Do not leave either your room or car unlocked as you transfer belongings. Have your room key in hand whenever exiting or entering your room; do not linger at the door or fumble around in your purse trying to find it. If someone seems to be loitering or following you, do not go to your room. Head for the front office and report it immediately.

If you have children with you when you travel, never let them run off to other parts of the hotel or motel area without a parent—not even to go back to the room to get something or to the pool or amusement area. All children, regardless of age or maturity, are at special jeopardy in these situations because there are so many transients on the loose.

Teenagers, in particular, may be at risk with "new found friends" they meet while traveling. Caution them against going off with others or bringing them back to your room. Ask them to socialize in public areas of the hotel, motel, or resort. Insist that they let you know where they are going to be, who they are going to be with, and when you can expect them to return.

Business Conferences

If you are attending a seminar or business meeting, it is best to stay at the conference hotel. The rooms there may be more expensive than surrounding hotels and motels, but you will save on transportation costs and it will reduce your chances of victimization while on the streets of a strange city.

When you venture out, do so in groups, and remove name badges that identify you as conference participants. Street criminals look for these badges or conference carrier bags to target out-of-towners. Also get good directions from the front desk on the safest routes to take.

Meet with business associates in the lobby or a restaurant. Just because someone is attending the same meeting as you are does not mean that person is not a threat to your safety. One woman was invited to have lunch with a seminar leader, a well-respected doctor in his field, who asked if they could stop by his room on the way so he could pick up something. She innocently went along, only to be sexually accosted by him as soon as they got to his room.

Safe Trips

Invest some time in preparing for any trip. A little planning up front can make your travels more enjoyable and safer, and it can help you avoid crises when you are far from home. You will not end up lost or find yourself staying in a bad part of town if you do your homework before you leave.

Learn as much as you can about your destination and the safest routes to reach it. Obtain maps and traveler's information through whatever sources are available to you—auto clubs, chambers of commerce, libraries, and the police departments in the areas where you will stay.

If you are going to another country, check with the Department of State on whether travel advisories have been issued about serious health or security conditions. Keep in mind that tourists are favorite targets of criminals.

If you require medications, take along an ample supply. If you wear glasses, bring along a spare pair. Anything that impairs your health sets you up as a more likely target for crime.

Carefully consider what you will pack. Do not take more clothing than you need and then end up hauling heavy luggage and loading yourself down—that only makes you more vulnerable as you travel. Stick with multi-purpose outfits and bring along at least one good pair of walking shoes.

Do not pack anything that you cannot afford to lose or have stolen. Leave the valuable jewelry behind along with unnecessary credit cards and irreplaceable family objects. Bring travelers checks and one or two major credit cards instead of cash.

Put your name, address, and home telephone number inside each piece of luggage you take. On the outside, use covered luggage tags and only put your name and a telephone number where you can be reached at your destination.

Keep in mind that soft-side luggage can be cut open, so hard cases provide better security. Choose pieces that have built-in rollers or bring along a luggage carrier with wheels to better handle the transport of your suitcases. Never leave luggage unattended, and make sure all your luggage pieces are locked.

Any critical items, such as medication and valuables, should be packed in a carry-on bag or tote, and keep that with you at all times. Make sure this bag has a sturdy strap that can be worn diagonally across your chest for better distribution of the weight and greater security.

Dress conservatively when you travel—you do not want to appear affluent, which attracts thieves, or look too casual, which announces "tourist." Resist discussing your travel plans or other personal matters with strangers, and be wary of anyone who approaches you offering to be your guide or show you where the bargains are. Also, never accept food or drink from a stranger—it could be drugged.

Keep in mind that when you travel, you are at greatest jeopardy in subway and train stations, airports, elevators and stairwells, tourist sites, market or festival areas, and the marginal sections of cities. Especially in some foreign countries, being a liberated, independent American woman makes you easy prey if you are traveling alone. Be on alert and stay with groups as much as possible.

Travel Itinerary

Leave a detailed travel schedule with family or friends at home so that they know where you are supposed to be and they can contact you in an emergency. Then check in periodically with them as your trip progresses. If for any reason you change your plans while traveling, be sure to notify them. The travel itinerary should list the dates and places you will be, the names of contacts, and the addresses and phone numbers of lodgings.

Make two photocopy sets of all your important documents for the trip—driver's license, airline or train tickets, passport identification page, hotel reservations, travel orders or authorizations from your employer, credit cards, and the list of serial numbers for your traveler's checks.

Leave one set of photocopies behind with your itinerary. Take the other set along with you, but put it in a secure place separate from your valuables. As you cash travelers checks, cross those numbers off your list. Bring extra passport photos with you to make it easier to get a replacement passport if yours is lost or stolen.

Public Transportation

If you commute to work, public transportation may be less expensive or less stressful than driving yourself. You may not own a car, and public transportation may be your only means of getting around. When you are on business travel or vacation, you may have to avail yourself of the public transportation system in the location you are visiting. Any mode of public transportation poses some safety risks, but there are precautions you can take to better protect yourself from crime.

Buses

Bus stations can be hotbeds of criminal activity, and you are more vulnerable if you fall asleep while waiting in the station or on the bus. If you are going to wait for a bus, pick the stops that are frequently used and in well-lighted areas if at night. It is always best to wait for a bus with other people around. Familiarize yourself with schedules so you arrive shortly before departure and you are not waiting around for extended periods.

When boarding a bus, have the exact fare ready. This is no time to be fumbling in your purse or showing others how much money you have in your wallet. The safest place to sit is near the driver, but away from the door. Some thieves will board a bus, grab a purse while still on the steps, and jump off before the doors close. Choose an aisle seat so you can more easily get up and move if you do not like the looks or attitude of the person in the seat next to you.

If anyone bothers you while you are on the bus, loudly warn the person off to draw attention, so other passengers are aware. Then tell the driver. Look outside before you get off at your destination in case there is a rowdy group at that stop or some other threatening situation; if so, stay on the bus. Also, pay attention to who gets off the bus with you. If anyone makes you uncomfortable or seems to be following you, head immediately to a busy place where there are other people.

Subways and Trains

When traveling on the subway or a train, have the money readily available to pay for fares or tickets so you are not opening and closing your purse in public. Map out your route and any transfers so you know ahead of time how to get where you are going.

Do not enter poorly lit tunnels or stairwells alone; try to move with a flow of people to your subway or train platform. Choose the middle cars where there are more passengers. Do not sit in the first or last car unless you have no other choice, and never enter an empty subway or train car alone. If you take a commuter train, and your stop is isolated or usually deserted when you arrive, have someone meet you when you get there.

Robbery at train or subway stations is not uncommon. You might be sandwiched between two accomplices on a platform. So be on guard. If someone tries to block your way or presses you from behind, move quickly to get away.

You are also vulnerable to theft or attack on longer train trips that involve overnight excursions, especially in foreign countries. Whenever possible, lock your compartment, and make sure your valuables and luggage are secured.

Taxis and Rental Cars

It is always best to use licensed company taxis since the drivers have to check in with dispatchers and the trips are recorded. These cabs will have company markings and a cab number. Call ahead or ask your hotel or motel to arrange for a taxi and get the approximate cost for the trip.

Beware of irregular cabs and independent drivers that cruise the streets looking for passengers; there is no central office monitoring their actions. Note the name and license number of your driver when you enter the cab. Tell the driver you will need a receipt, and that the name of the driver and the cab number need to be legible.

If you know the route you want to take, give the taxi driver your instructions. That shows you know the area, are a forceful person, and it separates you from the tourist trade.

When you rent a car, pick a model that is commonly available in the area you will be visiting and try to rent from a company that does not identify its cars as rentals. Some criminals go after tourists in rental cars. Get directions and go over your map while you are still in the rental car office so you do not end up lost and easy prey.

Before you drive off, make sure the car is in good repair and that all the locks work. Also, check the windshield wiper and washer operation. A vehicle with power locks and power windows gives the driver more control over the security of the vehicle. In warm climates, an air conditioner increases safety because it allows you to keep your windows closed.

Do not leave valuables in the rental car. If you are carrying luggage or purchases from shopping, keep them out of sight and locked in the trunk. Luggage in the back seat or hanging garment bags mark you as an out-of-town traveler and an easy mark.

Keep the car doors locked at all times. Put your purse on the floor of the car. Some thieves will grab purses through open windows when you stop. Others may just smash the window and reach in.

Air Travel

If you drive to an airport with your own car, use valet parking if it is available to you. That way you will be dropped off at your airline departure area and picked up when you return. That saves you from walking through poorly secured airport parking lots with luggage weighing you down.

If you are going to be away for more than a few days, either have someone drive you to and from the airport or take an airport limo or taxi. Your car is more likely to be stolen when left for a long period in a large parking lot.

Once you get to the terminal, keep a single tote or carry-on bag with valuables and "must-have" items in it with you at all times—airport lockers can be easily broken into. This single bag may need to get you through a day or so at your destination if your checked luggage is lost or delayed.

If you meet someone on a flight or have a particularly enjoyable seat mate that you strike up a conversation with, do not give out specifics of your travel plans or specific personal information. Be cautious if you are invited to do something with your new acquaintance when you arrive at your destination. Some people may just be friendly and hospitable, but others may have ulterior motives.

Held Hostage

Although hostage situations are rare, they can happen. An unstable person or a group might enter a public conveyance with weapons in hand. The best course of action in this type of situation is inaction—remain calm and keep a low profile.

Do not call undue attention to yourself by acting panicked, getting hysterical, or offering resistance. Cooperate and do as you are told, especially if a robbery is involved.

If a hostage situation continues for an extended period, ask for what you need in a level voice, such as food, drink, or a bathroom break, assuming reasonable requests will be met.

Key Points To Remember

- Plan your lodgings and get guaranteed reservations.
- Use valet parking or a secure garage recommended by the hotel.
- Always go over security measures with hotel staff when you first arrive.
- Keep valuables in the hotel safe and get a receipt.
- Ensure that all windows and doors are locked.

- Use a travel lock or door stop wedge for added security when you are in the room.
- Never admit anyone to your room without getting positive identification first.
- For motels, always park as close to your room as possible.
- Never leave your children unattended in hotels or motels.
- Caution teenagers against going off with new acquaintances or bringing them back to your room.
- When attending business meetings, stay at conference hotels and travel in groups.
- When traveling, learn about your destination and plan safe routes.
- Pack the essentials, but leave valuable items behind.
- Never publicize your travel plans, not at home or to strangers.
- Be careful of food and drink, and be on extra alert in tourist areas.
- Leave a detailed travel itinerary with a trusted person and check in periodically.
- Always have fares ready for public transportation and know your routes.
- Choose bus stops that are well-lighted and frequently used, and take a seat near the driver.
- Transfer and wait for buses where there are other people; avoid isolated areas.
- Do not enter empty subway or train cars alone.
- Use licensed cab companies and give taxi drivers specific instructions.

- Ensure rental cars are in good repair and not identified as rentals.
- Keep car doors locked at all times and valuables out of sight.
- Take an airport taxi or limo, or use valet parking for your car.
- Keep a single carry-on bag of essentials with you at all times.
- In a hostage situation, remain calm and cooperate.

Practice Scenarios

What if... ?

Someone knocks on your door and says hotel management has sent him to check the climate control unit.

You are shown to a ground floor motel unit and the patio sliding door has just a standard latch.

A man you have met at a business conference invites you to "discover the town" with him.

A man sitting next to you at the airport asks where you are coming from, your final destination, and how long you expect to be away.

A young man who was watching you on the bus gets off at your stop and starts following close behind you.

Three youths get on your commuter train and one pulls a gun and orders everyone to put their valuables in the knapsacks his companions are holding.

9

Safe at Work

Audrey had agreed to work an extra 2 hours to finish payroll. It was 7 p.m. and she noticed a few cars still parked in the lot below as she glanced out the third story office window, so it looked like there were others in the large office building still at work. She rubbed her eyes, grabbed her purse, and tucked the office supplies catalog under her arm—she would try to make up a list of items to order after dinner at home. She stepped into the elevator and noted two young guys in workmen's clothes, a bit unusual she thought for a white collar area. One of them asked her what floor she wanted. She said, "Ground level, please," and did not notice that he hit the basement level, instead. She did not realize she was in trouble until the doors opened and one of the guys grabbed her by her arm and pushed her out. She was beaten and robbed. The two guys quickly found the car in the lot that fit the keys in her bag, and they took off in her new car.

Understanding Security Measures

Your best defense against crime at work is to be aware of any security measures offered by your employer and to take

Safe at Work

More women than ever are in the workforce today, and unfortunately the workplace is a prime arena for crimes that run the gamut from invasion of privacy to murder. In fact, homicide was the leading cause of occupational death from injury for women over the last decade. You need to guard against petty theft, unwanted sexual advances, and outright assault. Hundreds of thousands of people are assaulted while on the job each year.

Keep in mind that your personnel record at work has a lot of information about you. Make sure you understand the personnel policies of your employer and your rights, especially to privacy. Check your record periodically to see what is contained in it and what others may have access to, with or without your knowledge. A young woman was recently stabbed in her apartment 2 weeks after moving in and starting a new job. The coworker responsible, who had developed a "fixation" on her, looked up the address in her file.

Pay attention to information provided to you by your employer on security measures, both to safeguard yourself and your work. If the information is not offered, ask. You need to know what kind of security is available. Are there security patrols? If so, when and where? Is there a security office you would call in an emergency? What are the hours of coverage, and what is the phone number? Post it in a prominent place; you do not want to be fumbling around for a number if you are in jeopardy. Call the number and ask what the response time would be to a call for help.

If security is provided by the building management or a private firm that handles an industrial or office complex, rather than your employer, ask the security firm how they screen applicants for jobs as security guards. You want to make sure they are there to protect you, and that you do not need protection from them. A security uniform does not automatically confer trustworthiness on the wearer. Be sure you know what the firm's security uniforms look like, too. This will prevent someone showing up in a rented uniform from gaining entrance on the pretext of being "security."

Find out which police precinct covers your place of employment. Call and ask what the crime history is for your area and your building. Ask about response times to calls for help. Be prepared to call security and/or police whenever you notice suspicious people at your place of employment, or if you feel you are in jeopardy in any way. Ask that a patrol be sent over to check things out.

You also need to understand how to secure personal valuables and work records. Are you allowed to have locking desk drawers, file cabinets, or lockers? Does your computer have a security code or personal password to protect your files? Who else in your organization has duplicate keys or a record of your code or password?

Discuss with coworkers and observe a strict policy of protecting each other by not giving out personal information to anyone who asks, especially over the phone. Never provide the home phone or address of an employee or disclose that a person is on vacation or on business travel. You could be setting that person up for a crime.

Just because someone claims to be a spouse, a friend, or a legitimate business acquaintance, does not mean it is true. Suggest that you take a message of the name and number of the caller and you will relay it to the person. If the caller persists, simply say, "I'm not able to provide you with that information."

In the same way that you should safeguard entry to your home, question the authenticity of any maintenance, repair, building construction, or delivery service personnel asking for admittance to the office. Ask for the name, company, and purpose of their visit and check it out before allowing someone access to secured areas and other employees at your worksite.

If you are in and out of your job site, attending meetings or dealing with customers, be sure that someone knows where you are going, how you can be contacted, and when to expect your return. When you are going to be "on the road," set up regular call-in times to report your progress and location. If you have a secretary or receptionist, let that person be the coordinator of this information. Otherwise, partner up with someone else at work to keep tabs on each other. If you do not return within a reasonable time or fail to check-in as planned, someone should be notified.

Evaluate with other coworkers any security deficiencies that exist at your place of employment. Put your request for additional security measures, such as more lighting, locking offices, better visitor control, and increased security patrols, in writing to the organization responsibile for security. Identify concerns and ask that employees be advised of any criminal activity that occurs at the worksite. Keep a record of the response. If the organization responsible for security is negligent or unresponsive, you could have grounds for a lawsuit if someone at work is victimized as a result.

Psychological Safety

Sometimes, violence on the job occurs because an employee is unstable and troubled or under the influence of alcohol or drugs. There are also incidences of disgruntled employees who have been fired, returning to the workplace with gun in hand. When people are stressed, hostile, or out of control, their behavior can be volatile.

Avoid confrontations with coworkers. If you cannot rationally discuss a dispute with another worker, ask for third-party arbitration. A supervisor or employee counselor may be able to mediate and find a solution acceptable to all. If you are concerned about the emotional state or behavior of a fellow employee, take it up in private with that person's supervisor. Sometimes, official intervention in a caring way can avert potentially dangerous actions on the part of distressed employees.

If you are a supervisor or manager, try to keep the emotional climate at the workplace one that is conducive to productivity and less likely to engender violent reactions to changing priorities or uncertain economic situations. You can do this by developing effective interpersonal skills in yourself and your staff, maintaining a calm and professional approach to the problems of employees, and showing sensitivity and support in helping them work through difficult situations.

Safeguarding Valuables

Whether or not you trust your fellow employees, most workplaces have visitors in the course of a business day, and they may or may not be monitored. If you leave your purse on your desktop, on the floor, on or under a counter near you, or anywhere else that is in plain sight or not secured, you are inviting trouble. A favorite "hiding" place is a lower drawer of your desk, but unless it is locked at all times with the key in your possession, this is the first place that a would-be thief will look. Keep your purse and other valuables locked up.

Do not leave anything you cannot afford to part with in unsecured lockers or common closets, especially credit cards, cash, or keys in your coat pockets. Small electronics have a way of "growing legs" when left out in work spaces, especially tape recorders, CD players, radios, and calculators. If you have a portable laptop computer or electronic diary or address organizer, they need to be secured to prevent theft. All of these items should be put away in locked drawers or cabinets whenever you are away from your work area.

Avoiding Assault

Physical assaults are more likely to occur both in isolated locations in basements, storage rooms, loading docks, or connecting corridors and in public areas where visitors might be, such as elevators, stairwells, rest rooms, and parking garages. Try never to be in a stairwell or any other isolated area alone.

In an elevator, always stand near the control panel. Look at the elevator panel and note the location of the emergency alarm button. If you are ever attacked or in jeopardy, hit this button and yell that you are being attacked and the direction the elevator is heading—either up or down. The emergency button usually activates a communication system and the monitors will hear you.

Another approach if something happens that you think is potentially dangerous, is to hit all the buttons immediately, and get off as soon as it stops. Also, if someone enters who makes you feel uncomfortable or is drunk or high on drugs, get off immediately. The same is true if you are about to enter an elevator; do not go in.

Realize that rest rooms are not a safe haven. You could be followed into a women's rest room by a man, especially if it is in an out-of-the-way area and does not require a key for entry. Try to use the more frequented facilities in the main areas of the work site. This is especially important when you are working late at night or alone and your building employs an after-hours cleaning service. If you work in a facility where there are all kinds of strange traffic in the vicinity of the women's rest room, set up prearranged "rest room breaks" and go with other women employees at the same time.

Parking garages, decks, and lots in office and industrial areas can attract a variety of criminals. There are numerous cases of women being attacked and killed in robbery attempts as they went to their cars at the end of the workday, especially on payday. Try to leave with coworkers. If for some reason your car is parked in a secluded area, ask that a fellow worker drive you to your car when leaving for the day.

You might want to set up a buddy system with another woman employee for this purpose—both of you going to one car and then driving to the other vehicle. If you have a security service, ask for an escort to your car. Do not be ashamed of being safety-conscious in these circumstances—it is smart behavior, given the reality of crime in the 1990s.

Working Late, Working Alone

You are more susceptible to crime at night or in the early morning hours and when you are alone, so whether you are a shift worker or a professional putting in long hours, you need to be extra alert at these times and take precautions to protect yourself and decrease your vulnerability.

Try not to work alone. Arrange to partner with another person for the same shift or if overtime work is required. Ask if you can do the work at home rather than alone late at night in an office. If you are going to get into the office extra early to catch up on work, see if you can get someone else to agree to come in at the same time. If you work in a store, either retail or a convenience store, ask that two people always be present on a single shift, especially at night.

If you are forced to work alone, then set up a check-in system with a friend or family member to regularly touch base and ensure you are okay. Let that person know the number of security or the police to call if you do not check in as prearranged. If you will be in an office with a door that locks, then lock it. If not, keep the door closed and wedge a doorstop under it from the inside to prevent the door from being opened from the outside.

Do not order dinner in from a delivery service for one—that only advertises your whereabouts and vulnerability. If you know you are going to be working late, pack a cooler with food and drink for the evening hours. It is a good idea, even if you have a vending area at work—these are not safe locations after normal business hours.

When you get ready to leave, let someone know you are leaving and where you will be going if you are making any stops on the way home. Give an approximate time for your expected arrival. If you can arrange for a security escort as you leave, do it.

Sexual Harassment

More places of employment are beginning to sponsor training sessions so that both men and women better understand the nature and effects of sexual harassment and requirements under the law.

If you are on the receiving end or directly affected by unwanted sexual advances, requests for sexual favors, or physical actions or verbal communications that are intimidating or offensive, then you are experiencing sexual harassment. Unfortunately, it is fairly common in the workplace, and women who are most economically dependent on their jobs are most vulnerable.

As people become more sensitized to the reality of sexual harassment, they are less likely to respond inappropriately to one another and more likely to build the necessary skills for deflecting unwanted sexual attention. You do not have to "go along to get along," nor do you have to create scenes to make your point that you do not welcome unsolicited sexual overtures or degrading sexual comments. The first course, of inaction, does nothing to change the situation; the second may only worsen your case and your cause.

Learn to be assertive so you are clear about your own position in any of these situations. Traditionally, women have not been adept at defusing inappropriate behavior on the part of the men they work with. You need to communicate your feelings in a straightforward manner without challenging the ego of the man or embarrassing him. For example, you can say, "I feel uncomfortable when you rub my shoulder. I would appreciate it if you wouldn't touch me like that anymore." Or you could say, "I don't believe in getting sexually involved on the job; it's bad business." If you are married, simply state, "I love my husband and I believe in fidelity in marriage."

One technique that can have more impact than verbally standing your ground is to write a letter to the offender and send it registered with a return receipt requested. In your letter describe the behavior that concerns you, state its effect on your ability to do your job, and ask that the behavior stop immediately. This keeps it between the two of you, but puts the person on notice that you are serious, and there is a good chance the person will back off without you having to file formal charges.

If the person who is pursuing or upsetting you does not get the message and persists or if you are penalized in some way at work for rebuffing advances, then you need to take it up through channels with a formal complaint. Any conduct that unreasonably interferes with your work performance should be addressed.

Your employer should acknowledge your concerns, counsel the harasser, and take appropriate action to alleviate the situation. If this does not happen, you can elevate your complaint to the Equal Employment Opportunity Commission (EEOC) under Title VII of the Civil Rights Act.

The strongest case you can make for yourself is to keep a log or diary that documents all incidents of sexual harassment if you are either dealing with a repeat offender or someone who is creating similar problems for more than one woman in your workplace. Describe each incident, including your response or reaction, as well as the date, time, place, and names of any witnesses. This provides evidence if you have to raise the issue with your employer, the EEOC, or in court.

A record of incidents can also help substantiate your claim for unemployment insurance if you are dismissed and your employer denies allegations or if you decide to involve the media and "go public." Always consult an attorney with experience in such matters for your own protection. Some women have been hurt in their careers by pursuing a sexual harassment complaint.

High-Risk Jobs

Some jobs by their very nature put you at greater risk of crime. If you work in either highly public areas or as an isolated individual, you may be targeted. Convenience store workers are at high risk, but they are less likely to be victims of robbery when there are two clerks on duty at all times.

If there are valuables at your place of business—large sums of cash, jewelry, electronics—such as banks and the retail trade in general, you may be caught in robbery attempts, and guns could be used. If your safety would be improved with bullet-proof enclosures wherever you work, you should make a strong case that your employer consider that option.

When making bank deposits, it is best to take two people and vary the times of deposit. Do not carry the deposit in a bank bag as this only advertises to prospective thieves that it is a deposit.

Just as you should not risk your personal safety to protect property when confronted by a mugger, your best course of action as an employee is to cooperate with robbers and get it over with as quickly as possible with your life intact. You can report the crime immediately after and will be able to give a better description of what happened if you remain calm.

Although the following examples are jobs that can be especially vulnerable, the advice given could be applied to any career choice that has similar circumstances. Use your judgment on how to adapt these approaches to your own work situation.

Business Owners

You are vulnerable if you are a woman business owner, especially in a service or retail business where expensive equipment, merchandise, or large sums of cash on hand are involved. Get to know the police that cover your area; ask that they check in on your establishment when you are there alone at night. Have the police do a security audit of your business site and correct any weaknesses; this is a business expense you cannot afford to ignore.

Keep display windows attractive but simple; do not place expensive items on display as a temptation to thieves or obstruct the view inside from the street so criminals can operate under cover. Keep the total amount in cash registers to a set limit and transfer excess funds to another secure location, but never in the view of customers. You might want to consider using a "dummy" safe with a reasonable stash to satisfy a robber, while actually keeping business proceeds in another hidden safe.

Women Executives

Any affluent career woman could be singled out as a target by virtue of the wealthy appearance of her lifestyle—the luxury car she drives, expensive clothing and jewelry, and an upscale home with costly furnishings. These things are irresistible to criminals.

Your business success does not garner you any special protection from crime and may put you at greater jeopardy. That is why it is important that you are alert at all times and take the extra precautions detailed in this book. High-visibility executives of companies may be at increased risk. Discuss additional security provisions that your employer can and should provide, including providing you with a bodyguard, if need be.

Teachers

With the alarming increase of violence in the schools, teachers as well as students are prime targets. In many inner-city schools where crime is so rampant that teachers and students are daily under siege, basic survival may be at stake. Maintaining control and sufficient discipline for actual learning to take place presents a major challenge. However, effective communications, clear school policies on disciplinary action, and a calm, respective approach to explaining expectations and reinforcing positive behaviors can go a long way toward maintaining order in the classroom.

Still, teachers may be subject to both verbal and physical abuse, and the more violent the school environment, the more likely you are to be assaulted. A clear, confident stance as a woman teacher will serve you as well in the classroom as on the street in protecting yourself against crime. Take a course in assertiveness skills so you can learn how to establish limits, communicate them effectively, and provide feedback to students without getting into confrontations or a battle of wills where you lose control or a student loses face. You also need to learn to combat group intimidation in case some students decide to join forces and are out to get you.

If you have been threatened or feel that you are in jeopardy from one or more students, report this to both the school administrators and the local police. Then take extra precautions and be aware, practicing the methods discussed in this book. Stick with other teachers and avoid being alone in secluded areas of the school, especially after normal school hours. Make sure your car is parked close to the school and in a highly visible location. Put your family on alert as well; sometimes irate students target the home of a teacher.

Health Care Workers

Women in the helping professions, especially those who work at hospitals, are particularly vulnerable to attack. They may work odd shifts or the hospital may be located in a high-crime area and the patients themselves are often capable of assault. More than half of the assaults at hospitals occur in the emergency room and the patients may be the violent perpetrators.

Crime in hospitals is on the rise, including theft, armed robbery, assaults, and even murder, and both the medical staff and patients are the victims. Unfortunately, hospital security forces have not increased accordingly.

Criminals have decided that these large institutions with so many transients and vulnerable patients in unlocked rooms are easy pickings. The hospital also has an arsenal of drugs, with an undeniable appeal for drug abusers. The turnover rate of hospital employees is high, and background checks may not keep pace, so it is possible that some employees may have criminal records.

It is important to lobby for effective security measures, and to constantly revisit the need for protective services with the hospital administration. Policies and procedures should be in place for dealing with disruptive and violent patients or the people who accompany them. Do not attend to a patient who has a weapon—get the police to confiscate it first.

Learn to recognize the signs of a violence-prone person—angry tone of voice or rapid speech, fidgeting or pacing, threats or demand for attention, delusional or paranoid behavior. You can help defuse a situation by explaining delays to people in the waiting rooms so they do not think they are being ignored.

Be careful to remove any item from your person that could be used as a weapon when you are dealing with either an agitated patient or someone threatening who has accompanied the patient. Remember, helping profession or not, you have the right to defend yourself and use reasonable force if you are attacked.

Real Estate Sales

Real estate agents are very vulnerable to crime, and they need to include safe practices into their daily sales strategies. One top seller in a Northeast city went off to show houses to a man who walked into the office and told her he only had that one day to find a house to relocate his family to because his employer was transferring him into the area. They later found her body stuffed in the closet of a vacant house she had just put on the market. The man had clubbed her from behind, stolen all her jewelry, and taken off in her late model Cadillac.

It is important to pre-qualify a person and get the prospect's full name, address, and phone number on your first meeting. Ask to see a driver's license, jot down the number, and leave it with the office manager. Never agree to meet a stranger at a property for the first time, and be suspicious of anyone demanding an immediate showing.

Do not make judgments based on appearances, but if someone makes you feel uneasy, take another agent with you to a showing. It is far better to show a home or hold an open house with a person along that you trust, although this might not always be practical. Always drive your own car and keep the keys on your person. Keep your prospects in front of you when showing a house so you can watch them and not be taken by surprise from the back.

Certain prospects are more likely to pose a threat to you as an individual agent—a single man, a group of adults, or any individual who is not willing to give you the information you ask for. You are also at greater risk when showing properties in remote areas, high-crime districts, or that are unoccupied, especially if the electricity is off. Leave the flashy jewelry and other valuables at home; they are a liability on the job.

Always leave information at your office when you go on showings as to who your prospects are, what properties you are showing, and when you can be expected to return. Set up a system of regular check-ins when you are going on long showings or handling an open house. Partner with another agent if you go prospecting door-to-door and for open houses, if at all possible. Carry a cellular phone with an easy 911 or other emergency number access.

Flight Attendants

Flight attendants are at particular risk for unwanted attention from passengers. In addition, they travel all over the place, staying in hotels and shared apartments. Women in the hospitality business, airborne or otherwise, are often considered fair game, so they need to learn assertive skills to deflect unwanted advances. They also need to be careful about socializing with passengers. An up-in-the-air attraction could end in a dangerous down-on-the-ground date. As with meeting any stranger, charming or otherwise, pick a public place to meet and do not go off alone or otherwise make yourself vulnerable to attack.

Key Points To Remember

- Understand security measures offered by your employer.
- Check your personnel record and know who has access to it.
- Find out which police precinct covers your place of employment.
- Secure your personal valuables and work records.
- Never give out personal information on employees to callers.
- Monitor access to secure areas by visitors and repair people.

- Let your office know your destinations and schedules when you travel outside the office.
- Put requests for additional security measures or safety concerns in writing to the organization responsible for security at your worksite.
- Be sensitive to the emotional climate at work; avoid confrontations with coworkers.
- Stay out of isolated locations at the workplace when you are alone.
- Always stand near the control panel in an elevator, and get off immediately if you feel uncomfortable with other riders.
- Use the more frequented rest rooms in the main areas of the worksite.
- Walk out with other employees to your car at the end of the day.
- Avoid working late unless there are other employees with you.
- If you have to work late alone, check in with someone regarding your schedule and whereabouts.
- Be assertive about unwanted sexual attention at work.
- Keep a record if there are repeated incidences of sexual harassment.
- Women in high-risk jobs should discuss safety precautions with their employers and take common-sense steps to safeguard themselves.

Practice Scenarios

What if... ?

A man from "security" shows up in your reception area and says he needs to do a "walk-through" to ensure that valuables are secured.

A sales representative calls and asks for the home address of an employee so he can send her a thank-you gift for her business.

An employee who was acting stressed-out is put on involuntary leave, and he returns brandishing a gun, vowing to "get even."

You are taking the stairwell to the basement when you hear footsteps coming fast behind you.

A company manager comments on how you look, tells you dirty jokes, and rubs up against you every chance he gets.

The elevator doors open, and a guy gets on with you who smells of beer and fixes you with a glazed look.

10

Avoiding Sexual Assault

Patricia was delighted to meet a new man at her friend's dinner party who seemed so together. John was attractive, bright, and an up-and-coming real estate developer. He told her how great she looked, and asked her out for dinner the following weekend. He offered to drive her home after the party. On the way to her apartment, he said he had to stop by his own place to check for an important phone call he was expecting. He invited her to see the great view from his condo while he went through his messages. Patricia was admiring the view, when an iron grip grabbed her upper arm and propelled her through the bedroom door. The next thing she knew, she was pinned beneath his bulk as he tore at her clothes in spite of her protests. He kept telling her how good it was going to be, covering her mouth with alcoholic kisses, as he pushed into her. She was stunned, shocked, trembling at the suddenness of the attack. She could not believe that this had happened. John rolled off of her. "Thanks. We'll have to do this again. Now, you should go home," he said, dismissing her.

Defining Sexual Crimes

Since sexual crimes are primarily committed against women, women are more aware of and concerned about these types of crimes, and rightly so. This concern stems from being inherently vulnerable to generally more physically powerful men in a society that encourages men toward aggressive behavior.

Fear of rape is part of the female consciousness in a pervasive way from puberty on. It is hard for men to understand or relate to it in their own world view of crime, even though they are concerned about female loved ones. There simply is nothing equivalent to it in the general male experience.

Sexual crimes are the only crimes where the victims are often blamed or considered a party to their own victimization, sometimes by themselves as well as by others.

Every woman has the right to view her body as her own possession, to insist this is respected by others, and to protect herself against potentially dangerous situations. Learn to assert yourself and clearly set limits with men so that passiveness or poor communications do not permit misread messages by members of the opposite sex.

Sexual assault is a crime of violence. It is about power—the ability of the perpetrator to dominate or humiliate the victim. There may be some distinctions between stranger rapes and rapes by known assailants, but respect is lacking in all cases. Often the act is an expression of rage against all women or one in particular.

Rapists come from all walks of life; they are frequently married, and may otherwise lead normal lives. They may even have all the outside trappings of success and respectability. However, they are unstable, frustrated, or insecure. They use the sexual act to vent their hostility, degrade, or prove their "superiority" over the victim. When a man physically forces himself on a woman, that is an act of aggression and personal violation.

The legal definitions of sexual assault crimes, such as molestation, rape, sodomy, and oral copulation differ, but the emotional trauma caused by these crimes is the same. The trauma can last for months or years, long after the attack is over and any physical injuries have healed. These crimes affect not only the victim, but the victim's family and relationships, current and future. They can affect a person, either physically or psychologically, for life.

Preventing Sexual Assault

The first step in prevention is to understand that you could be a victim of sexual assault, and that this is a prevalent crime in our society. One out of every four women will be raped in her lifetime, although the vast majority of these rapes will go unreported. Of course, this means that the rapists are free to rape again, and they will. Many rapists rape over and over until they are caught.

There are no "protective" factors for this crime—not age, race, physical unattractiveness, marriage, pregnancy, motherhood, economic status, or type of employment. All females are at risk. Rape victims come from all walks of life and range in age from infants to women in their 80s and 90s.

Although women worry most about stranger attacks, they are really at greater risk of being sexually assaulted by someone they know. Understanding situations that put you at risk for acquaintance rape, learning to set boundaries with the men you interact with, and recognizing danger signs that should put you on full alert will help protect you from sexual assault by men that you meet or are involved with.

Stranger Rape

Some rapists plan ahead and may target several women in the same neighborhood. Others are opportunists looking for vulnerable women to attack. In either case, the rapist does not want to be interrupted or caught. He is likely to choose remote or deserted areas, if outside, or homes and apartments that are easy to enter with lone occupants.

The steps you can take for home and car security as well as personal safety in your everyday activities that are discussed throughout this book can also help safeguard you against sexual assault from strangers.

Women in their 20s and 30s are not the only rape victims, and it is a mistake for middle-aged women to think they are immune. In fact, women in their 40s and early 50s are frequent rape victims. These women are in the same age range of the mothers of the most active age group of ambush-rapists and burglars, men in their late teens and early 20s.

Trying to dismiss or scold a potential attacker who is younger may only provoke the hostility that the assailant has against his own mother, a stepmother, or other female authority figure who may have verbally or physically abused him. He can transfer his rage or resentment to you.

Another group of women at high risk is those women who are in the same age range as their assailants. Younger women are out socializing, exploring their newly independent selves, and they may not be as cautious or concerned about their vulnerability, until they become victims. Then it is too late.

Safe behaviors need to be reinforced in all women. Women are particularly vulnerable to surprise attack through lack of awareness or a failure to trust their instincts. They should be cautious of potentially dangerous situations and not charge ahead because of a misplaced sense of either politeness or bravado.

Be especially wary of men who offer help when none is needed, are not easily rebuffed, try to charm you or imply instant rapport, give you too many details about themselves to assure you during an initial meeting, make promises about their motives, accuse you of rudeness to get your cooperation, or enlist your aid to get you away from other people or to a more remote location.

Acquaintance Rape

The vast majority of acquaintance rape victims are women between the ages of 15 and 25, although the victims of this crime can be any age and come from all social and economic classes. College freshmen are particularly vulnerable. For many, it is the first time away from home. They may be overly trusting of dates as part of the campus community. They may also be flattered by the attentions of upper classmen who maneuver them into compromising situations.

The best prevention against this crime is to be cautious about men you are meeting and do not know well, both in private and professional settings. Try meeting men in public places either for dates or business discussions. Do not readily give out your home phone or address until you can trust the person.

Never go off alone in a car with a man you just met, or to your place or his. Most acquaintance rapes occur either in the car or at a secluded site that the victim has been driven to, or at the home of either the assailant or victim.

Just because you have been dating a man or you know him through work, community activities, or mutual friends does not mean that he is incapable of sexual assault. Drinking or drugs may lower inhibitions, or he may think he is entitled to sex because he has spent money on a date.

You may be in an isolated situation with him when he starts to get sexually aggressive. This is no time for mixed messages. As soon as you detect the intent, you need to clearly set limits and not allow him beyond your boundaries. Stop the momentum before it gets out of hand.

It is critical that you recognize the danger signals and verbally assert yourself. If you have been drinking to excess or using drugs, you may not recognize the danger signals until the attack is on. You probably will not be in good condition to fend off the attack, either.

Does a man have the right to take advantage of a woman's inebriated state? Absolutely not. Does a woman's poor judgment either to drink too much or as a result of drinking put her at risk of rape? Absolutely. You can argue the social injustices of this situation, but the woman who ignores this advice is in great danger.

If he tells you that he is interested in having sex, and you are not, say so—and clearly. Do not insult him, though, especially if he has been drinking. Verbal attacks on your part will challenge him to prove something and may provoke his underlying rage or insecurity.

Just say, "I don't know you well enough to be intimate," or "I don't believe in casual sex." If he tests your boundaries by touching you to see what he can get away with and how you react, call him on it. Say, "Take your hand off my thigh. I'm not comfortable about this. Don't touch me that way."

It is also important to remove yourself from the situation, or at least from being alone with a potential assailant. If you are at a party, get back to where the crowd is. If you have driven yourself to a place where you met him, then use an excuse and get out of there. If you were driven by your date, be sure to always have enough money to call a cab and get yourself home so you are not dependent on him for transportation.

If you are alone with him or in an isolated location, try to talk your way out of the situation, even if you have to imply that "next time" might be different. Tell him you have an infection and cannot have sex until it clears up. After you get away from him, you can ensure there will not be a next time.

If you are aware of the potential of certain character traits to predispose a man toward sexual violence and abuse of his partner, you can screen out these men before you get too involved with them. Having a long-term relationship with this type of person will put you at a high risk of danger. Look for these signs:

- Does he anger easily and overreact to little frustrations, lashing out at people and things?
- Does he exhibit wild mood swings—charming and up one moment, nasty and down the next?
- Does he brood over slights, carry grudges, and glare when someone irritates him?
- Is his language hostile or contemptuous when referring to women in general or you in particular?
- Is he selfish and insensitive, disregarding your feelings or beliefs, or belittling your ideas?
- Is he controlling of all aspects of your behavior, telling you how to act, dress, or think?
- Is he extremely possessive and jealous?
- Does he ever get "too physical" with you? Does he have a history of violent behavior?
- Does he expect to get what he wants and bend others to his will? Is he inflexible?
- Is he a drug or alcohol abuser?

Gang Rape

Gang rape is really about male bonding and that is why offenders are normally members of a group—a fraternity, an athletic team, a military unit, bikers, or a street crew. The victim is a woman as "object," the men taking turns sexually assaulting and debasing her, insensitive to her pleas or protests.

The male group will rationalize its actions, the members supporting each other. Even if all do not participate, no one will stop the rape. They will dismiss the woman as a "slut," or tell themselves that "she wanted it" or somehow "deserved" what she got.

Often, the victim is "set up" by one member of the group. He will pay her attention, get her drinking, and then find a way to isolate her from others. If it is at a party, he may invite her to a room away from the crowd. Once there, his buddies show up and the attack begins.

Almost invariably, when gang rape occurs, whether planned in advance or opportunistic, there are drugs or alcohol involved. Intoxication serves to reduce the control and rational thinking of the men and impair the judgment of the hapless victim.

Men may be able to drink with their friends and not worry about being violated; women cannot afford to follow this behavior. **If you are drunk or high, it will affect your ability to assess dangerous situations and reduce your powers to effectively safeguard yourself.** It may not be fair that men can party without the same consequences, but it is reality. You need to recognize this to avoid becoming a victim.

Whenever you are in a situation where men greatly outnumber women and alcohol consumption is high, you are at risk. Stay where the crowd is or stick with a girlfriend, and watch your own alcohol intake. Drink from unopened bottles and cans and be careful of any "spiked" special that is being offered; you will not know what is in it or what effect it can have on you. Leave the party before the situation deteriorates into a bunch of prowling drunks.

If you are ever accosted by a group of men, try to determine who the leader is and address your verbal self-defense to him. There is usually one person who encourages the group to perpetrate the sexual assault. The others usually would not commit such a crime on their own. Your best bet for averting the situation is to deter the leader.

Obsessions

There are several types of individuals with obsessions:

Peeping Toms can be curious adolescents or obsessed adults. You can usually discourage this kind of behavior by keeping your blinds closed and good outside lighting on at night. If you become aware of one in your neighborhood or someone tries to make contact with you by leaving a note or calling, notify the police. This type of behavior is usually harmless, although disturbing, but someone may go over the line and decide to pursue the fantasies he is having about you.

Exhibitionists derive their satisfaction from exposing themselves and the shock this evokes. They do not usually attack victims. Stay calm and move away. Then call the police to report the incident, describing the person and giving the time and location.

Stalkers are another situation entirely. They may shadow their victims for weeks or months and call or send notes describing their fantasies or making threats. A stalker can be a former lover or ex-husband, a coworker, a neighbor, an acquaintance whose overtures you rejected, or a complete stranger who has a fixation on you.

The trouble with stalkers is that they may plan to or spontaneously move to take action when an opportunity presents itself, and they can catch you alone. Stalkers have perpetrated a variety of crimes against their victims—destroying property, killing pets, rape, beatings, and even disfigurement or murder.

Whether they mean to consummate a relationship that only exists in their head or do you harm for your real or imagined rejection, stalkers mean trouble. **Get the police involved immediately**. You may decide to file for a restraining order through the courts. If so, generally it is better to do this sooner, rather than after the situation escalates.

Let friends, family, and coworkers know about the situation. You do not want them inadvertently helping the stalker by giving out personal information. Document each time you are followed or contacted by the person. Tape record, photograph, or videotape encounters. Get a second unlisted phone number for friends and family to use, and put an answering machine on your original phone number to record threats made by the stalker.

You will also need to switch into your extra alert mode. Try to alter your routine and schedule on a day-to-day basis so the stalker cannot easily follow you. Avoid situations where you can be isolated. Usually, the most effective strategy is to break all contact with the stalker, especially if you were formerly involved. Talking or meeting with the offender gives him access to you and only puts you in greater jeopardy. Make whatever changes you can to put you out of the stalker's reach.

Resisting Rape

Unfortunately, there is no single all-purpose approach to warding off a rape attempt. What might work in one sexual assault situation with a particular attacker, could make matters worse or be totally ineffective in another situation with a different assailant.

Much depends on the individual motivation of the rapist, the personality of the victim, and the circumstances surrounding the attack. The time and location of the assault, as well as your opportunities for help or escape, are important elements of the equation. You might also have to consider jeopardy to others; for example, if you had a small child with you when assaulted.

However, this is one area where advance preparation and mental rehearsal can really pay off. You need to understand the possible mindsets of rapists, evaluate your personal abilities and limitations, and consider possible responses and ways to overcome an attack.

If you do this, you will be better positioned to confront an actual assault with a calm mind, use your wits, and determine your best course of action. In fact, studies show that women who effectively deter sexual assaults use several different strategies in combination.

It is normal to experience fear when you realize that you are in jeopardy, but it is your reason and ingenuity that will help you best cope with a rape situation. You need to recover as quickly as you can so you can assess your assailant and your situation.

Most women react in one of two ways to sexual assault—anger, which is much more conducive to action and active resistance, or panic, which can immobilize the victim. The first group is more likely to have rape avoidance as the goal; the second group fears injury or death, and these women are more likely to acquiesce in the rape.

Unfortunately, women who do nothing are not spared—certainly not from rape, and in many instances, not from further brutality and sometimes even murder. Keep in mind that this is a power play fueled by hostility. A victim mentality can serve to reinforce the assailant's need to degrade the victim. It is for this reason that begging, pleading, and crying are the least effective responses to an attack.

Sometimes, being passive may be the only alternative you have. Your personal makeup may prevent you from actively resisting. Your assailant has a weapon and you do not feel that you could effectively fight him. You are trying to protect others.

No one can tell you whether active resistance is best, but studies of effective rape resisters have shown that the women who successfully thwarted an attack used several different approaches—fleeing or trying to flee, yelling or screaming, fighting back. Some techniques for defending yourself are presented later in this book. There are pros and cons to each.

Keep in mind, though, that once you decide on physical resistance, there is no turning back. You may decide that this is an immediate reaction or a last resort. In either instance, it helps to have surprise and speed on your side, so you might pretend cooperation temporarily. However, if you decide to fight, you must be willing and able to inflict serious injury on your assailant. The goal is to incapacitate him so you can get away.

If your assailant has a weapon, you have to make a judgment call. Although fewer women used the more forceful strategies when the rapist had a weapon, the ones that resisted did increase their chances of avoiding rape. Resistance often resulted in injuries such as bruises and scratches, but not resisting was no guarantee that injuries would not occur.

If someone with a weapon is trying to force you into a car, this is a very dangerous situation. Once he drives you away, usually far from help, anything can happen. You can try to scream, run, or fight back or you could use a ploy and pretend to faint. When your body goes limp and he puts both hands on you to try to drag you into the car, he does not have control of the weapon. Then you can try to fight or flee.

Whenever immediate physical resistance is out of the question, you can pretend cooperation. Try to get your assailant to put his weapon aside, and wait until you can create the chance to fight back or escape.

Other strategies have been recommended to women in the past, such as tell him you have a disease or make yourself vomit, with the hope that the assailant will drop the attack out of fear or disgust. Sometimes women are advised to talk to their assailants and try to persuade them not to continue the attack. However, studies of women who successfully resisted attack showed that reasoning or pleading with an assailant were not usually effective in deterring stranger rapes.

That does not mean you should not try to communicate with your assailant. You might be able to lower an assailant's guard by conversing with him calmly. Do not antagonize him. If you can think of a way to stroke his ego, you might be able to defuse your attacker's anger, divert his attention, or negotiate terms. Meanwhile, you can consider your options for escape.

One woman told her assailant that she was staying at a nearby hotel and they could go there and be more comfortable. Once inside the hotel lobby, she screamed her head off and the man was apprehended. Another woman asked her attacker to set up a "date" for later in the evening at her place, and when he arrived, the police were waiting.

If you are at home, you might try to convince your attacker that your boyfriend or husband will be home soon and it would be best if he left. Of course, these performances need to be convincing. If you do not have enough actress in you to deal with a crisis situation in this way, then ploys such as these will not work for you.

Surviving Rape

The aftermath of rape can be devastating. Women feel defiled and their first inclination may be to clean up. Resist the impulse; this can destroy evidence that will help establish a case against your assailant.

Report the sexual assault immediately to the police or a rape crisis center. You can decide later whether to file a complaint against the rapist and prosecute the case in court if he is charged. Remember, though, that a rapist is a repeat offender; he will go on to rape others unless he is stopped.

Go to the nearest hospital emergency room for a medical exam. Do not bathe, brush your teeth, douche, or change clothes. Preserve all physical evidence until the hospital has completed the exam. Bring a family member or friend with you or ask that a rape counselor be present. It is important to follow up with counseling to help with the feelings of helplessness, loss of control, fear, shame, and anger that rape evoke.

Domestic Violence

Victims of domestic violence come from all cultures, religions, ages, and economic classes. What they share is a sense of helplessness, shame, and isolation. Yet few will admit their situation to friends, family, or the police. Some do not even admit it to themselves. Much of the abuser's power to continue assaults relies on this denial and secrecy.

Although anyone in a household may be a victim of domestic violence, it is usually the woman. More than 2 million women are battered by their husbands and lovers each year, accounting for over a third of all hospital emergency room visits by women. What is more, the FBI reports that half of all women murdered in the United States die at the hands of husbands and lovers who have lost control.

Domestic violence operates on a cycle of abuse, with a period of tension, the battering incident, and then a period of remorse and guilt when the abuser is apologetic, affectionate, and loving. Because the woman loves the man, fears abandonment, or is financially dependent on him, she forgives him, hoping that it will not happen again.

However, over time, the abuse becomes more frequent and severe. The man may be jealous, possessive, and controlling, forcing her to have sex against her will and threatening her and the children. Understanding the dynamic of this abusive cycle at the beginning and seeking help is the best defense.

Assault, even by family members, is a crime. Seek medical attention for all injuries, and ask the hospital staff to include a photograph of your injuries in your medical record in case you decide to seek legal action. Report the incident to the police or sheriff's office. Ask your families to encourage your husband to seek help for his violent behavior through counseling and support groups.

Getting away from the abuser is your smartest strategy. Find out about battered women shelters or other agencies that can provide help. If you can plan your escape, put aside money, and decide on a place to go, fine. If you think that you or your children are in danger, leave immediately. Battered women's shelter locations are secret and they provide the best place to be safe. They have a wealth of experience and information for women in your situation.

Key Points To Remember

- Sexual assault in any form is a crime of aggression and violence.
- The perpetrator wants to vent hostility, degrade, or prove superiority over the victim.
- The victim can experience severe physical and/or emotional trauma.
- Women are more at risk of rape by an acquaintance than by a stranger.
- Be cautious and practice safe behaviors to reduce risk of assault.
- Never go off alone with a man you do not know well and trust.
- Excessive drinking or drugs impairs your judgment and increases your risk of sexual assault.
- Clearly set sexual limits and boundaries with the men you date.
- Beware of controlling men with short fuses who do not respect your wishes.
- Avoid male group situations where drinking occurs and women are outnumbered or you are isolated from the crowd.
- Keep your blinds closed and never change clothes in front of a window.
- Ignore an exhibitionist and keep moving.
- Immediately report any stalker to the police and keep a record of incidences.
- Only you can decide how to respond to sexual assault given the circumstances, your assailant, and your own personality.

- Women who successfully resist rape usually employ several strategies to deter the attack.
- Begging, pleading, and crying with an assailant are the least effective responses.
- Some women have outsmarted their assailants enough to deter the attack or escape.
- Victims of rape need to preserve evidence until a medical exam is completed and should seek counseling and support to recover from the trauma.
- Women are the most frequent victims of domestic violence, and the abuse escalates over time.
- Intervention is needed to break the cycle of domestic violence; both the abuser and the victim can benefit from counseling and support.

Practice Scenarios

What if... ?

You leave a bar and you notice a young guy is following you to your car.

You come back from a first date with a new man, and as soon as you sit on the couch to have a cup of coffee, he lunges at you.

The party you are at is winding down and you cannot find your girlfriend or the boy that invited you.

You keep seeing the same man turning up wherever you go. He never says anything to you, but he watches you intently.

Twice now, your boyfriend has hit you for not behaving the way he thinks you should. He apologizes the next day for drinking too much and losing his cool.

11

Protecting Children from Crime

Lucy was in the back running through the sprinkler in her bathing suit when her mother last checked on her. The little girl splashed the cat as it went by and then chased it around the side of the house out to the front yard near the mail box. The cat took off across the road and Lucy knew not to cross the road, so she just stood there calling back the cat. A car pulled up with a man and woman inside and asked what she was doing. She told them in her lisping 3-year-old voice that her cat had run off. The nice people said they had kittens at their house and they would be glad to take her to get one, so she climbed in and sat between the two people. The next time she would be brought back to her house by police would be 5 years later after being abandoned at a rest stop on a highway three states away from her home.

Practices and Precautions

In a world rampant with broken homes, drug and alcohol abuse, and deteriorating value systems, violent crime is on the upswing, especially among youths. Some of the pressures that today's children have to contend with are more intense and very different from those experienced by their parents. That is why open communication is especially critical between parents and children.

Parents need to do more listening, if they are going to comprehend and help deal with the challenges their children face. Understanding the issues that affect your children daily will help you to better prepare them to protect themselves. Certain child protection principles have repeatedly been shown to be effective in certain situations, and they can serve as a security umbrella for your children at any age.

The single most important thing that you can do to safeguard your children is to provide a good example. Children are great observers and imitators. If you practice the personal safety techniques explained in this book, if you show your concern for security in your home and in your car, eventually your children will pick up these safe behaviors. Children learn by watching and by doing.

You can help reinforce personal safety habits in your children through a variety of ways that will be discussed, but you need to be safety-conscious yourself first. Not only is this critical for building credibility with your children, but if you are careless about security issues and personal safety, you put your children at greater risk for being victimized along with you.

This means teaching them to always lock doors and windows, not an easy task for children who may be running in and out to play. Take them around the house with you to see that the doors are locked and the windows are closed and locked.

They also need to learn to look through peepholes and not to open doors for strangers or even people they know if they were not expected. You will most likely need to have a step stool nearby for your children to use. You could have a house rule that children under a certain age must allow an adult to open the door for a caller, especially at night.

Make sure they lock up their bikes or other valuable playthings, rather than leaving them lying around the yard. You can help them through the process, but do not do it for them. You are trying to instill good safety habits as a natural part of their day-to-day activities.

Emphasize the specifics of what your children can do to safeguard themselves in positive terms. You want to encourage them to safe behaviors, not frighten them about all the "bad" people that are out there waiting to do them harm.

Tell your children that although most people are decent and want to protect children, there are a few people who are not. These people might hurt them, and that is why they need to be careful and to "think safety" so they can learn to protect themselves.

Several other approaches will greatly increase the personal safety of your children. **You should always know the whereabouts of your children.** Keep track of them and insist that they stay in touch with you. Make it clear that you trust them to stick with their plans, and you expect them to call you if there is any change in plans.

Whenever there is a change in who they will be with, where they are going, what they are doing, or when they will be home, they need to tell you. That should be a house rule. Even if your children are playing at the next door neighbor's house, do not let them migrate another door down to some other child's home without notifying you.

Be sure to "check it out." Whenever your child is involved in an organized activity or going to a friend's house, get the details and verify them with the adult who will be in charge—either the group leader or the other parents.

Children should not be "dropped off" the first time they are involved in an activity. Go in and preview a club meeting, stay through a game, go to the home of the friend. You need to assess each situation to ensure that there are adequate controls, that safety is taken seriously, and that sufficient and trustworthy adult supervision is being provided. You may have special concerns that need to be addressed.

Impress upon your children that there is safety in numbers. They will be far safer if they travel in pairs or if they stay with a group. Some places where there are often many people, such as beaches or parks, are not as safe as they once were, but your children are still better off if they do not allow themselves to be separated from the crowd.

You can teach your children that if they are ever threatened or in trouble, the best course of action is to head for other people and ask for help. They should yell as loud as they can, "I don't know this man. He is trying to hurt me." If anyone tries to grab them, tell your kids to run as fast as they can and scream for as long as they can to create a ruckus and attract the attention of others.

Have your children learn their name, full address, and telephone number with area code as early as possible. Make a game of it. Put the information on cardboard cutouts and use these as flash cards. Make sure they know this information by heart.

Also teach them about 911 or any other emergency number for your area. Unplug a phone set and have them practice in your presence until they get it right. Then have an emergency drill. Pretend that someone is trying to get into the house. Have them call the 911 number on the disconnected phone and explain the problem to the imaginary dispatcher on the other end.

Point out the location of public telephones in your area, and have your children practice making phone calls on a public telephone. Ensure that your children always carry enough change on them when they are out to use one in an emergency. Tell them that they can always dial "O" for the operator and ask to be connected to the police—even without any money.

If you have a cellular phone in your car, let your children practice using that as well. At the rate that this technology is developing, it may not be long before we can equip our children with small, personal cellular phone units to stay in touch. Some parents have given older children paging units; however, many schools have outlawed pagers on school grounds because of their use in illegal drug deals.

Safe Walking Routes

Familiarize and orient your children with the immediate area where you live. You can do this when you take short car trips to run errands. It is critical to "walk the walk" with your children in your own neighborhood as soon as they are old enough to understand your instructions and pick out landmarks.

Count the number of houses from the nearest cross street to your home. If there is a police or fire station, take your child into the facility for a visit, and explain that this is a good place to go if they are ever in jeopardy. When you get back from your walk, draw a map of the area with your children and have their "fingers do the walking" to go over the route you took.

Try to connect with neighbors to set up a safety net of "emergency" houses where children can go for help if they get locked out of their own homes, are being bothered by older kids, or need to get away from strangers that approach them.

You might be able to set up reciprocal agreements with the parents of other children in your community. If there is a retired couple nearby you are friendly with, you might ask the couple to be "surrogate grandparents" for your children.

Let your children know they should run to the nearest such "safe house" if they need aid. These informal networks not only provide crime resistance and backup support for children, they can be the source of babysitter pools and a way to share local community news and issues.

If your child regularly walks to school, determine the route and then walk it together a few times to see how long it takes. Note if there are special concerns based on what else is happening along the route during certain times.

Reinforce that the child is not to hang around the school after hours or take a short-cut that might be risky. If you agree on the route that should be followed and you know the time required, then you can project the time you would expect for your child to arrive at school and return home.

Children walking alone are at great risk. Try to arrange for two or more children to walk together. Forbid them to accept rides from anyone without your prior approval. Tell them to advise the school and you of any strangers that approach them along the way.

Consider driving the child to and from the school yourself to ensure safe passage. You might be able to work out a rotational car pool with the parents of other walkers.

Bus Riders

If your child rides the bus to school, waiting alone at a bus stop is risky unless you have your child in sight the whole time. If at all possible, have your child wait with others, either at your own stop or the next closest one, or you might want to wait in your car with your child until the bus comes.

Go over the steps that are necessary to ensure the bus is made on time. Also discuss a backup plan with your child if the bus is missed for some reason, either going to school in the morning or returning home in the afternoon.

One mother had to leave for work before her daughter's bus arrived. When the 10-year-old child missed her bus one morning, she decided to walk the 3 miles to school. A woman who commuted along that route each day saw the young girl walking along the road and was concerned for her safety, so she offered her a ride to school.

The woman also gave the young girl her name and phone number to give to her mother and offered to be a backup ride if the girl ever missed her bus again. This was a nice gesture from a stranger—and the girl and her mother were lucky.

The story could have had a different ending if someone who did not have the girl's welfare at heart had come along. The mother had never discussed a contingency plan for a missed bus, so she put her daughter at risk. Also, the girl put herself at further risk—she should never have gotten into the car of a stranger.

Abduction Prevention

A staggering 1.3 million American children are abducted or missing each year. The majority of these children are runaways or are kidnapped by the parent who does not have full custody after divorce, but some are abducted by strangers.

Of these stranger-abductions, two-thirds involve sexual assault, and children of all ages are targets for pornography and prostitution. Some 150 children that are abducted end up dead.

A majority of these abductions occur on the street or in other public places when a child is isolated, lured away from others on some pretext, or taken by force. You see the faces of missing children on mailers and posters. What can you do to ensure your child is not one of them?

First, understand the nature of the crime. Child molesters come from all walks of life and they are repeat offenders, with many victims. They develop approaches for luring children that work over and over again.

Studies show that children who are neglected or unhappy are more vulnerable. Children who are loners are more easily separated from groups of children. If they are deprived of parental attention, they are more likely to respond to an adult's offer of fun, money, or companionship.

Sometimes molesters will play on the sympathy of a child and ask the child to help find a lost pet, or say a parent is hurt and they have been sent to pick up the child. Do not put your child's name on clothing or other items in a visible location; a stranger that can call your child by name may catch the child off guard.

Younger children are easier marks. They simply do not understand the danger when approached by a friendly stranger and may readily cooperate with a request. They are not good at recognizing deception.

Children in the 8-10 year age range are a little more savvy about overtures made by strangers and not as easily tempted, but they are still susceptible. **Children should be told never to accept gifts from a stranger or go off with someone into a car or away from others.**

If someone approaches your children or asks them to go somewhere, they should know to immediately get away and go tell their parents. Make it clear that you would never send a stranger to pick them up, even if you were hurt.

They also need to understand that a "stranger" is not just a mean looking man—it could be a handsome, friendly man, a woman, or even a teenager—anyone they do not know.

Insist that your childrens' schools call the parents of any children that do not show up for school in the morning. The same thing should hold true for day care or after-school care. Also, check immediately on any delay in the trip home.

Set up procedures with the school and any day care or after-school care center about releasing your child to anyone but yourself, and let your child know what those arrangements are. If someone other than a parent regularly picks a child up, provide the center with a photograph for easy identification.

Tell your children that if anyone says their parents have sent them to pick them up, your children should immediately run back into the school or center and check this out.

The best way to teach your children to respond in an appropriate way and react quickly to an abduction attempt is through repetition of "what if" scenarios. Several of these scenarios are provided at the end of this chapter for your use.

If someone approaches your child and asks a question, the best response in most circumstances is to ignore the person and get away. You do not want your child engaging in conversation or happily going off with someone. If a child is being followed or chased, then help should be sought where there are other people.

Older children, if asked directions, should know to stand back, never going to the car to be helpful. Adults should not be seeking instructions from children anyway. Teach your children to keep walking and say, "I can't help you. You'll have to ask another adult."

If the car continues to follow along, your child should immediately turn around and run in the direction opposite of where the car is heading. That way the driver must turn the vehicle around to continue to follow, and it gives your child a chance to go for help where there are other people.

Another danger is if your child is ever separated from you in a public place, such as a mall or an amusement park. Each time you go someplace, reinforce the need to stick together. It only takes a few seconds for your child to be out of your sight and suddenly gone.

Discuss what to do if your child gets lost. Either tell the child to stay put, not to wander off in search of you, or point out a "safe" person to go to for help, for example, a woman sales clerk or attendant, a security guard, or a police officer.

You might want to create a "child identification card" to place in your child's pocket or pin to the inside of clothing for whenever you go out. Just use a 3x5 inch index card. Give your child's name, address, phone number, and age, parents'names, and any special medical information, such as blood type, medications, allergies.

You can also bring along two current pictures of your child whenever you are going to be in a crowded area or at a public event in case you get separated. That way, you will have one photo to give to police or security guards and one photo that you can show to other people that may have seen your child.

While you do not want to dwell on the possibility of abduction and scare your child, tell your children that, if they were ever separated from you, you would continue to look for them no matter how long it took. Often an abductor will try to manipulate the child, saying the parents do not want the child anymore. To combat this, they need the powerful reassurance that you love them and would not rest until they were found.

Tell your children that if they are ever taken away they should look for opportunities to escape. If the abductor takes a child into a fast food restaurant, for instance, the child should wait until inside and then yell, "This man is kidnapping me. He is not my father!"

Your children should also know that if they can get to a phone away from the abductor, they should call 911 and tell the dispatcher that a kidnapper has them and they need to be rescued. Your child can either give the number of the phone being used or hold on long enough so the police can trace the call.

Rehearsals and Reinforcements

Once your children enter school, they will most likely take part in classroom-based prevention programs. Sometimes these programs are worked into the normal teaching situation; other times, special programs may be conducted by local police. However, you cannot wait until a child is 6 or 7 years old to address crime prevention issues.

Much younger children can be targets of crime. You need to develop personal safety skills in these children to prevent abduction as well as sexual abuse by a family member or known adult, which unfortunately is more likely than abduction by a stranger.

How do you do this in a child who does not read and is not articulate enough to be able to discuss or even recognize dangerous situations? Children are naive and friendly naturally, so you need to carefully define for them what a stranger is. Just because they have seen someone around does not mean he is a friend.

Keep the concept simple. Draw a circle and put some stick people inside the circle. Name a few close friends and family members as the stick people. These are the "insiders." Other people are "outsiders." Outsiders are people that your child does not know well, such as neighbors or the mail carrier, and people that your child does not know at all. If they are not inside the circle, they are strangers.

Do a show and tell as much as possible. There are some coloring books on the market that can help parents address safety issues in simple terms, but these alone will have no lasting effect with young children. You really need to lead the child through the process and role-play situations. Play "let's pretend" and show the child exactly what is expected.

For example, if you tell your child to stay by your side and never get out of sight, that alone will not make an impression. The very first time you are out and your child's attention is drawn by something colorful, you will have a wanderer to track down.

Set up a make-believe shopping mall in your living room and put out items designed to distract your child in key locations. Then "walk" your child through the mall, looking at merchandise and testing his or her ability to stay with you.

Each time your child moves away from you or drops your hand, reinforce what is expected. Say, "No, we hold hands when we are in a store," or "No, I must always be able to touch you when we are out together." If you make it through a trial run, praise your child extravagantly, "You stayed close to Mommy the whole time. That is wonderful!"

Practice verbal scenarios and act them out with your child. Get other members of the family to play roles. Have someone be the "stranger" that comes up to your child playing in the yard and says, "Hi. I have a nice puppy for you in my car."

If the child does not fall for one lure, try another, and another. Most child molesters use several different approaches to get a child to go with them. In each case, your child needs to practice a standard three-part response: say "No," get away, and tell someone you trust what happened.

When you discuss "good" touching versus inappropriate "bad" touching, you can use a doll as a visual aid. Let your children know that it is not right for other people to touch their private areas, the parts of their body covered by their bathing suits, unless it is a doctor visit and you are present.

Go through different situations with the doll to show what is okay and what is not okay. Then show the child different circumstances and ask, "Would it be okay for Uncle John to hug the doll?" or "Would it be okay for the sitter to put her hand inside the doll's panties?"

In each instance, praise and reinforce the child when an appropriate answer is given. If the child misreads the situation, calmly discuss why it would or would not be okay. "When someone loves you, a hug is a good way to show it," or "That is your private area; other people should not touch you there."

Child Abuse

Sexual abuse and molestation of children is an alarming reality for many, with the Federal Bureau of Investigation (FBI) estimating that one out of four girls and one out of ten boys will be victims before their 18th birthday. Of the men who batter their wives, nearly three-quarters also batter their children. So spouse abuse is strongly associated with child abuse, which affects millions of children each year.

Obviously, children are least likely to be able to fend off attacks of any type because of their physical size and the ability of adults to intimidate them in other ways. The real tragedy is that they are more in jeopardy from the people they know than from complete strangers. This compounds any physical injury by the emotional damage done to innocent children who are betrayed sometimes by the very people who should be protecting them.

This is one area where awareness is of great importance. Women need to understand that their children can be victims, and they can be victimized by family members and friends. If it is a situation of domestic violence, things will not get better without intervention and counseling.

Monitor the interactions of other people with your children and confront unacceptable behavior or even discussions if you do not like what someone else is saying to your child. You also need to be open to your children and the way they respond to visitors in your home. If they are uncomfortable or sullen around a family member or friend, they may be responding to either a perceived threat or actual occurrence of improper conduct.

When the molester is known to the child, the child may be kept in line through bribes, threats, or fear of disclosure, especially if the child is too young to really understand what is happening. Keep in mind that the offender may be an adult that is admired by your child or could be another older child—either a family member or friend.

Some signs to be on the lookout for that might indicate your child is being sexually abused include: sudden behavior changes such as withdrawal or aggression; sleep disturbance and nightmares; regressive behavior and bedwetting; fear of certain people or situations; unusual interest in sexual matters; and pain, itching, or bleeding in the genital area.

Women need to be particularly sensitive to potential harm when they live with boyfriends who are not the natural fathers of their children, are part of blended families because of remarriage, or shuttle their children between two households because of divorce.

One woman lived with a man for 5 years before she found out he had been sexually abusing her 9-year-old daughter the entire time. He had told the girl he would kill her mother if she said anything. The girl finally confided in a school counselor when the man molested her 6-year-old sister in front of her while the mother was away on an overnight trip. The man was eventually jailed for these crimes, but both daughters sustained physical injuries and required years of therapy to deal with the emotional trauma.

Even young children should be taught that their bodies belong to themselves and they can say "no" to anything that makes them uncomfortable. They should never be forced to go along with the actions of others out of politeness. If they do not want to be kissed, or tickled, or juggled in someone's lap, that should be respected.

One woman's child steadfastly refused to climb into Santa's lap each Christmas at the mall to get her photo taken. "We do not have any photos of my daughter with Santa, " the mother said, "but my little girl knows she has the right to refuse something that makes her uncomfortable."

Children should also feel that they can tell their parents if someone does or says anything that disturbs them. If they do, they should be believed and not punished in any way. Reassure them that nothing bad will happen to them for telling you. There are no secrets from Mom or Dad. They should tell you immediately if anyone threatens them or asks them to keep a "special secret" that bothers them.

You should never respond in an angry or accusing way to such a revelation, no matter how disturbing. Remain calm, and let the child talk it out, describing the incident and expressing the fear. Listen, and comfort the child. Never confront the offender with the child present.

Many adults who were abused as children say that even worse than the actual offenses themselves was the failure of a trusted adult that they confided in to take action to protect them. In many instances, they were met by outright denial, blame, or attempts to discount the seriousness of the transgressions. Whether you take legal action or not, keep the child away from the offender while you decide what to do. There are crisis centers and child abuse hotlines that can help you to deal with the situation, but do not sweep it under the rug. Children who are believed and supported can heal over time so that the damage is not a lifelong legacy.

Telephone Talk

Young children should not be allowed to answer the telephone until they are mature enough to strictly follow family guidelines. They are too open and willing to give out information that could be used by unscrupulous callers.

All family members should answer the phone with a simple "Hello." Do not provide even the name of the family or the telephone number that has been reached. Wait for callers to identify themselves and state their purpose in calling, then either turn the call over to the appropriate family member or take a message.

A child should never admit to being alone or even state the whereabouts of the parents or other guardian. If callers do not identify themselves and start asking questions, family members should respond by asking "Who is calling, please," and ignore the questions. If a caller is persistent, say "I can't continue this call unless you identify yourself," and then hang up.

If a child is alone, or if the parents are there but busy, the child should be taught to say, "I'm sorry, she (he) can't come to the phone right now. May I take a message?" If the caller asks what the parent is doing or where the parent is, the child should just answer that the parent is "busy" and again repeat the offer to take a message. If a caller pursues it beyond this point, the child should hang up.

Just as child molesters use many ploys, so do criminals who use the phone as one of their tools. It is hard for children to see through the ploys and resist giving out information.

Again, you need to drill them on possible tactics and use "pretend" phone scenarios for preparation and practice.

To solicit information, a caller might say he is checking on an order a parent made, he has a delivery, or he is an old friend of the family. The child has to be taught to deflect all of these situations. Just say, "I can't give you any information. If you will leave your name and number, someone will call you back."

Also, teach your child to handle wrong numbers by asking callers for the number they were trying to reach. If it is not the family's phone number, just say, "Sorry, you have the wrong number." They should also know that if someone calls and says something obscene or scary, they should hang up immediately without saying a word, and then tell a parent.

Post important numbers by each phone in the house. This list should include the usual emergency phone numbers such as the police, fire department, and poison control center. Also add the names and numbers of family doctors, the parents' work numbers, and the numbers of trusted neighbors and family who could be called to help in various situations.

This list of numbers can be critical in an emergency situation because children can easily panic and forget phone numbers they already know.

Child Care Arrangements

Carefully screen anyone coming into your home and clearly state the ground rules and expectations for safe behaviors. It is not enough to leave some emergency phone numbers to contact you "in case." You need to thoroughly discuss security measures with any babysitter, even family members and close friends, including how to screen callers and unexpected visitors.

In many instances, the babysitter will be a young teen. Whether or not this teen is a responsible person, you cannot expect the maturity or experience in dealing with suspicious or dangerous situations that an adult might have.

Do not assume sitters will be able to handle all situations. Question them on different scenarios and see how they say they would react. What would they do first if there was a fire or a stranger knocked at the door? It is important to discuss such issues with babysitters to assure they would take appropriate action.

A sitter should never say "I'm just the sitter," when answering the phone, answer questions of telephone solicitors, or give out any information. Instruct the sitter to say you are unavailable at the moment and take a message. The sitter should also not be using your phone for personal chats while you are away. It is important to keep the line open.

You also need to be clear on whether a sitter is allowed any visitors. Sometimes two teens may want to team babysit for you, and you might find this acceptable. However, keep in mind that having a girlfriend or boyfriend over may distract your sitter from the primary responsibility of watching your children. It also opens your home to another person who might not be as trustworthy.

If you do allow the sitter a visitor or companion, be sure you have the name, address, and phone number for the other person as well as the primary sitter. As an extra precaution for someone you do not know, check the arrangement out with the parents of both young people.

When selecting a sitter for the first time, be sure to get personal recommendations from other parents or go to a local church or synagogue for referrals. Get some references and check them out, asking other parents what they thought of a particular babysitter.

The first time a sitter works for you, consider coming home on some pretext much earlier than you said you were, just to evaluate the situation. Catching the sitter unawares may reveal a lot.

You should always ask your children for specific feedback each time they are left in the care of others, and be sure your sitter knows that you do this. Say something like, "Have a good evening together. I know I'll hear all the details from the kids tomorrow."

You also have a responsibility to safeguard your sitter as well, so do not do anything that puts the sitter at additional risk. You will probably need to transport the sitter, or at least ensure escort to a car or public transportation. If you are dropping a teen off late at night, be sure that she can get into her home safely before driving off.

Always ask for a report on how the day or evening went and if there were any concerns. This will give you an account to compare with your children's version. Also, talking with the sitter in this way gives you a chance to reinforce acceptable behavior and attitudes and discuss and correct anything that disturbs you.

If you will be having someone come to your home regularly to care for your children while you work, be prepared to make careful background checks before making a decision. Ask for and follow up on personal references. You can even request that the caregiver be fingerprinted and have your local police ensure the person does not have a criminal record.

You might also insist that the person be trained in first aid and CPR, paying for the course yourself to ensure the person is certified. These precautions make sense in all instances, but they are especially important if the person will be caring for an infant or toddler.

Even if your child cannot talk, be alert to the way your child interacts with the caregiver and the type of behavior exhibited when the sitter is around. Ask the caregiver to keep a "daily log" of events and activities. You can use this as a convenient place to leave notes for each other as well.

Set the ground rules on whether the caregiver is allowed to take the children out of the home, and how to notify you if this is allowed. You should also go over security measures and safe behaviors when your caregiver is the guardian of your children in public places. Put your instructions and expectations in writing. That way there is no chance that you might misinterpret each other.

If you are going to place your child in family day care or a day care center, expect to do some homework before you make a choice because quality varies greatly. You should also be cautious because of news accounts across the country of sexual abuse in certain facilities.

Establish up front whether a day care provider is licensed, registered, or certified. Discuss how issues of discipline are handled, what security measures and safety policies are in place, and what the adult-to-child ratio is. All of these factors will affect how safe an environment you are placing your child in.

Get the names and numbers of other parents who have used the day care center and talk to them before enrolling a child. Turnover of staff is another issue. Unfortunately, child care is not a highly paid occupation and staff changes are unavoidable. However, ask what kind of screening is performed on employees before hiring.

You should be able to drop in unexpectedly at any time. If a day care provider tells you this is not allowed, look for another place to take your child. Regular visits to the day care provider will give you a good idea of how your children spend their days and can help you stay up on changes in routines or approaches. You will also get to know the staff better.

Ask your children to discuss their experiences and feelings. As long as you are getting positive feedback from these talks and the day care situation meets your other criteria, then it is a good match.

Parents sometimes ignore their own misgivings. If you see negative changes occurring in an operation or your children are unhappy with the arrangement or their caregivers, investigate other options. It is worth the trouble to make a change if it will better safeguard your child.

Missing Children

If you keep tabs on your kids and they are responsible about calling in, then you should know within a short span of time if they are not where they should be. If you suspect your child is missing, take action—**call the police immediately**.

After you contact the police, you can call friends and family and check along the route where your child should have been, as well. You will need to provide the complete circumstances of the disappearance. Ensure the police include the case in the FBI-operated National Crime Information Center computer for national availability.

If your child were to disappear, having accurate and current information about your child would help police and other agencies in their search and investigation. Putting this information together takes a minimal amount of time and can be done at low cost, but it would be critical if your child was ever missing. You need to update this information each year, to keep pace with the changes and growth in your child.

You can make up a child identification kit yourself by creating a personal data card on each child and including the following information: full name and nickname, date of birth, sex, blood type, height, weight, hair color, eye color, any distinguishing marks or characteristics, clothing and shoe size, health conditions, medications, and special interests/hobbies.

On another index card, tape a lock of hair and fingernail clippings from your child and put that in a small plastic bag. Collect a handwriting sample from your child if old enough to write. You should also fingerprint your child and include that in the kit. The last item needed is a set of color photographs of your child. Put all of this together in a file folder or large ziplock plastic bag and store the information in a safe place. You may want to use your camcorder at home to create an identification videotape of your child, as well.

Other information that could be used to help identify your child includes dental x-rays, medical injury x-rays, and eyeglass prescription and frame type. Make sure you obtain this information whenever you change health care providers or move.

The National Crime Prevention Council (800-288-3344) produces a McGruff® Safe Kids Identification Kit that provides information for parents and their children and includes a personal record form and fingerprinting materials.

Key Points To Remember

- Recognize that open communication is especially critical between parents and children.
- Take time to listen to your children, their ups and downs, who their friends are, and what is happening in their lives.
- Set a good example of safe behaviors and healthy lifestyle choices.
- Help your children to safeguard their own possessions.
- Always know the whereabouts of your children, and have them check in with you.
- Evaluate each new activity for a secure environment and proper supervision.
- Encourage your children to "stay with the crowd," and not to go off alone or with someone they do not know well.
- Teach your children their name, address, and phone number as early as possible and how to use the phone for emergency calls.
- Map out safe walking routes, time them, and show your children safe homes and other public places they can go to for help.

- Have your children wait with others for buses and work out a contingency plan for missed buses.
- Tell your children never to go off with someone they do not know well (on foot or in a car) or accept anything offered by strangers, and reinforce this by testing their responses to the ploys that child abductors use.
- Discuss what to do if your child is ever separated from you in a public place.
- Be alert to possible sexual or physical abuse by people your children know and trust; these are the most likely offenders. If your children confide in you, believe them.
- Teach your children how to screen phone callers, and tell them never to admit to being alone or to give out personal information over the phone.
- Carefully screen babysitters, family day care providers, and day care centers, and be sure to contact references.
- Put security concerns and safety procedures in writing and go over them with child care providers.
- Keep accurate information and a record of identifying features on each of your children in case they are ever missing.

Practice Scenarios

What if...?

A woman comes up to you at the park and asks you to help her find her puppy.

A handsome man says he will give you money and take you to the arcade.

A teenager offers to give you something "cool" that will make you feel real good.

A man says I have sent him to pick you up because I am too sick to drive.

We become separated at the mall.

You are walking down the street, and a car pulls over and the driver asks you for directions.

Your aunt's boyfriend is always tickling you, and he tells you he wants to share a "special secret."

12
Safety Concerns for Adolescents

Becky was a little lost again, not unusual for her first week as a freshman in high school. She wandered down a corridor in search of the media center, and then decided she must be on the wrong floor. As she rounded the corner, she saw three older boys lounging on the top steps of the stairway. "Excuse me," she said, "could you tell me how to get to the media center?" "Sure," one of the boys replied amiably, "but it's gonna cost ya." "Yeh," another boy said, "penalty points for getting lost." The third boy grabbed her ankle and yanked her to the ground, then all three fell on her pinching and probing her breasts and buttocks, passing her along a gauntlet line. "Not bad for a baby," one of them said. "Yeh, welcome to high school." The third reached into her book bag and extracted a change purse, emptying the contents in his hand. "Look," he said, "Mommy gave her cookie money." With that, they left, laughing among themselves, leaving her on the floor, crying.

Emerging Independence

Adolescents are more vulnerable both to becoming involved in crime and being the victim of crime as they deal with the insecurities that face this age group, their need to prove their independence and separate identity, and the enormous peer pressure to be "cool."

Alcohol and drugs are the greatest threat to the safety and future of the teen population. If the groundwork has not been set by parents at earlier ages, then this is the time youths will be most susceptible to the lures and dangers of abuse.

Children are never too young to discuss the dangers of tobacco, alcohol, and illegal drugs. The earlier you start, the longer you will have to reinforce positive health messages. You need to get to your children well before someone else does who will put them on a road to self-destruction.

Too many kids are carrying guns and knives, as well, so even slight provocations can end in tragedy between teens whose emotions are volatile. Firearm homicide is the second leading cause of death for teenagers 15 to 19 years of age. Many youths are exposed to other types of violence; in fact, someone 12-19 years old is twice as likely as an adult over age 25 to be victimized.

As if street and school crimes were not enough, adolescents may also be the victims of, or witnesses to, domestic violence. This barrage of violence takes its toll on the mental health of children in a variety of ways—anxiety, depression, aggression, and substance abuse. These additional problems only make the situation worse for the adolescents involved, and they may hurt themselves and others as a response to the suffering they feel.

Parents, schools, and health care professionals need to be sensitive to the reality of adolescent life in a violent society. Teaching youths safe and responsible behaviors is only part of the equation. The community may have to provide services to address violence-related psychological trauma for young people in this age group.

These young people are growing up in a world fraught with many more dangers than only a generation ago. Parents who are interested, involved, and supportive provide a strong influence for their teenage children in countering threats to their health and safety.

Parents should also work with the schools, community

groups, and the police in a reinforcing network to provide structured activities as an alternative to "hanging out." Young people who are left to their own devices can become part of the problem instead of part of the solution.

Numerous programs across the country that have involved youths in community activities have found that they can contribute to positive aspects of community life, while building respect and pride in their own accomplishments. One program called Youth as Resources (YAR), sponsored by the National Crime Prevention Council, offers small grants for community service projects carried out by young people with adult support. For information, call 202-466-6272, ext. 131.

Latchkey Kids

In a society where there are many single parents or both parents work, the question of "when can you leave a child home alone" is a critical one. Unfortunately, there is no answer that fits all situations.

Depending on what estimates you use, anywhere from 5 to 12 million children in this country between the ages of 5 and 13 years of age are regularly at home during some part of the day without adult supervision. Some of these children are left to care for younger brothers and sisters. Parents also need to determine when to leave a child home while running an errand, or at what age a child can be left alone at night while they attend an adult social event.

Few would contend that the average 14-15 year old is not mature enough to stay alone or babysit younger children. In fact, with many older teens seeking part-time outside employment, the babysitting pool available to parents these days consists mainly of 14-15 year olds.

However, early adolescence is a time of great turmoil. A child alone can be both lonely and afraid, and unsupervised youths of this age can get into trouble or easily be preyed on.

Young teens are no less likely to be abducted than smaller children, and may in fact be at greater risk.

It is far better for children not to be alone, certainly not at the younger ages, and ideally not even in early adolescence. Maturity levels aside, there are still the issues of judgment, experience, and security. A child, no matter how responsible, is not as well equipped as an adult to handle threatening situations.

Many school systems are beginning to respond to the need for supervised care by offering extended-day programs. If your child's school does not, and if your child cannot stay with a relative or trusted neighbor, explore other after-school programs at nearby day care centers or family day care homes. An arrangement can usually be worked out for bus transportation to the after-school care location.

One single mom of a young teen worked out an arrangement with another mom who worked from home and had two young children. The older girl went straight to the other family from school each day and watched the children for three hours while their mother worked in her home office. The teen's mother picked her up on her way home from work.

All benefitted from this arrangement. The older girl earned some money babysitting while giving the children's mother uninterrupted time, and the teen's mother did not have to worry about her daughter being home alone. In addition, the teen's self-esteem was enhanced by caring for the younger children, and the children delighted in her company while their mother was occupied.

What if you have no choice or are unable to make an arrangement so your children can be with others while you are out of the house? How do you leave children alone without anxiety? That is probably not possible. What you can do is reinforce their mature and responsible behavior, teach them skills that will enhance their self-reliance, and help them plan activities that can keep them occupied.

The younger the children, the more critical it is that you

work out ways to monitor them when they are home alone and to provide backup support for emergencies. Call them frequently or have them "check in" with you by phone when they arrive home. Also make arrangements so that either you—or someone else you trust—can be reached if they have questions about their safety or a crisis arises.

Make sure that someone responsible will always be available—at least by phone—to the child, if the child needs contact or advice. Children can get lonely, scared, or bored while home alone; they need some kind of support.

Neighborhood backup is critical. Some communities have set up special "warmlines" for latchkey children to call. This does not take the place of parental reassurance and contact, but it can offer your children an alternative source of adult support if they get concerned or need to talk to someone while they are by themselves. Find out if any of these services are available in your area.

Street Safety

If your child is going to be alone for any part of the day or evening or traveling alone getting to and from your home, you need to reinforce and apply some of the key safety messages that are addressed elsewhere in this book.

Discuss basic street safety. Your children need to know that if someone stops them and demands money or some other valuable, they should stay calm, give it up, and get away. As soon as they can, tell a policeman or you.

They should always walk with a group of people and keep their heads up and eyes open. Headset radio, cassette, or CD players should never be used on the street. They will not be able to hear what is going on around them, and small electronics are tempting items for thieves.

Tell them to avoid groups or gangs hanging out on the street and cross to the other side any time they have a "bad feeling" about anyone approaching them on the street. They also need to know if anyone offers them anything—cigarettes, alcohol, drugs, money, or other "gifts," they should calmly say no and keep walking.

Other Safety Issues

Children need to practice good key control. They should check each morning to ensure they have the house key before going out. If they carry the key on a chain around their neck, it should be kept out of sight, or kept in some other standard place that is handy but not visible to the casual observer. The key should not have a name or address on it, in case it is lost or stolen. If the key is lost, your children need a backup home they can go to until you come home.

If it looks like someone has broken into your home or is in it when they arrive, they need to know not to go in to investigate, but to head straight for a neighbor and call the police. If, when they arrive, everything looks okay, they should enter the home quickly, lock up immediately, and put the key in a safe place where they can find it the next morning.

Another critical issue that is a safety rather than a crime prevention concern is what to do in the event of fire. You really need to have home fire drills to give your children practice in the steps involved in dealing with this type of emergency and getting out quickly and alive.

Older children are better equipped to deal with the reality of a home fire. Younger children may panic and sometimes even hide from firefighters that are trying to rescue them. **Make sure every capable person in your home knows how to operate a fire extinguisher and keep one handy in the kitchen.** If you have family pets, it is important for your children to understand they must get out themselves and call for help. The firefighters can save the family pets.

Go over the telephone techniques provided in this book

and procedures for screening visitors at the door. Your children need to understand that under no circumstances should they ever admit to being home alone. Have them put lights on in more than one area of the house and keep a radio playing.

For younger children, it is probably best not to answer the door at all. If they are in secure homes with doors and windows locked and an alarm system on, they can look out the peephole but should say nothing. In most instances, the person will go away.

If a visitor persists outside the door or tries to gain entry into the house, your children should know to go to the designated safe room in your house, lock themselves in, and call the police so they can come and investigate. They can then call you or a nearby friend, relative, or neighbor who serves as your backup contact for emergencies.

House Rules

Establish house rules for what your children can and cannot do when you are not at home with them. It is a good idea to arrange for easy-to-prepare snacks. Young children (under the age of 12) should not be using a stove, toaster oven, or microwave without adult supervision.

Keep a first aid kit readily available and teach your children how to deal with simple injuries—a cut, a splinter, or a nose bleed—and what to do in a more serious health emergency. You also need to discuss their avoidance of dangerous things, such as matches, chemicals, medicines, knives, or guns.

Children may use their time alone to snoop through their parents belongings, so keep anything that you do not want them to have access to under lock.

Work out agreements in advance about how your children will spend their time—their responsibility to complete homework or chores, the type and duration of television watching or video games, talking on the phone with friends, or going anywhere or inviting anyone over without your permission.

There are no guarantees that your children will follow your instructions. However, if you are specific about what you expect and help them to structure their time, you greatly decrease the possibility that they will be hurt or get into trouble while you are not home.

School Security

Crimes in schools are on the increase, with both teachers and students as victims. According to one national crime survey of 26 big cities, more than 200,000 students and 50,000 teachers were victimized in a single year.

From the time children begin school, they need to be educated in the basics of personal safety. This cannot start too soon. Although middle and high school students are more at risk for incidents involving weapons, even elementary school students have been robbed, raped, and solicited for drugs.

Large sums of money and expensive athletic gear, including sports jackets and shoes, put the older child at risk for robbery and assault. Discourage taking valuables to school for this reason.

Disruptive incidents, personal violence, and theft occur mostly during regular school hours and are perpetrated by the students enrolled. Most students are attacked by other students, and they know the offenders. Middle school children and younger high school students seem to be most at risk.

According to the National Institute of Education, the safest places in schools are the classrooms. Students are more at risk between classes and when they are in corridors, stairs, rest rooms, cafeterias, gyms, and locker rooms. Your children need to be aware that lagging behind the crowd in any activity might put them at risk, so it is always a good idea to stick with companions.

You need to encourage your children to avoid trouble and situations that can erupt into violence at school. They need to understand that walking away from trouble, refusing to rise to someone else's bait, or using humor to defuse a situation is not cowardly behavior—it is smart.

They should recognize potentially dangerous situations:

- Stay away from rowdy groups of students.
- Do not crowd around an impending fight.
- Beware of rest rooms where one student is "standing guard" outside the door. Use rest rooms during normal breaks and go with friends.

Your children should feel they can confide in you about any dangerous situations they observe in school—other students with weapons, illicit drugs and alcohol on the school premises, outsiders or troublemakers that hang around school property and accost students. You do not want them to hide the reality of their school experience from you because you might be horrified or overreact.

Help them explore the best ways for them to handle situations themselves, although serious concerns should be reported to the school administration. Do not be too quick to intervene in personal situations which may involve one or two other students. Ask your children if they want your involvement first.

Your children will build both strength and confidence if they learn to evaluate a situation and effectively handle it, rather than being fearful or intimidated or always having a parent intercede. Having an "open ear" and guiding your children with empathy as they navigate their school years can help them to develop better skills for interacting with peers.

Keep aware of the problems, though. Many public schools are having to deal with weapon and drug problems that were unknown to the parents of the children attending these schools when they themselves were students. It is difficult to get a decent education when you are under siege.

Check with school officials on written policies for handling visitors, weapons, violence, students with a history of dangerous conduct, and sexual abuse. What are the controls over who can enter school grounds? How are background reviews conducted on school staff? What is the school's recent history on incidents of crime and violence?

Parents need to understand the reality of their child's school experience if they are going to help their child cope with the daily challenges of surviving unscathed. Working together as a community of parents, teachers, and students, you can address these problems, enhance the safety and welfare of the students, and improve the overall learning environment that the school provides.

Conflict Management

Many youths have a need for coping skills, especially conflict resolution and learning to deal with anger. Several studies have shown that violence is prevalent in the attitudes, beliefs, and actions of adolescents in this country. This sets up a pattern of aggression that results in gang fights, individual attacks, and sexual assault against young women by the youths they date. However, young people can be taught to alter their behavior.

Some schools have found ways to reduce risks and violent interactions with effective crime prevention programs incorporated in their curriculums. These programs teach alternative ways to work out differences. Young people can be shown more acceptable approaches for responding to real or imagined threats.

Check to see if your school system teaches conflict resolution and mediation skills. If not, you may be able to work with the Parent-Teacher Association, other community groups, and the police to bring these kinds of programs into the school.

Schools that have adopted these approaches have shown students that they can solve everyday conflicts without violence. These programs also encourage mutual respect among diverse student populations.

Conflict resolution and mediation skills not only help adolescents in dealing with others for school activities, they carry over into later life and their relations as adults.

Driving, Drinking, and Drugs

Communities across the United States have had to deal with the same tragedy—teen deaths in car accidents caused by operator error of a young driver. These accidents usually involve kids who were out partying. They were under the influence of alcohol or drugs, driving at excessive speeds, and often did not have their seat belts on. This combination of behavior represents the greatest danger that teens pose to themselves.

Teens are in an experimenting and rebellious stage. They are trying to distance themselves from parents to establish their own identity. Despite their protests, they are not as mature as they would like to appear. They still need limits imposed on their behavior, even as they rail against them.

A parent needs to be a continuing influence during this turbulent period. Be aware of the dangers and temptations that your teens are dealing with. If you have open communication, rather than shouting matches, you can help them better understand their choices in the face of peer pressure and realize the consequences of their actions before they end up a statistic.

Alcohol use is prevalent in this country, and it is available even to underage adolescents. Drug use is on the rise, and it starts at earlier ages than just a generation ago. You need to discuss the ramifications of substance abuse with your children, build their self-esteem, and expose them to activities in life that will "turn them on" safely and naturally.

Pretending these problems are not out there, ignoring the signs, and failing to discuss the realities of the teen social world in the 1990s will only put your children at greater risk. You have to tackle these issues head-on.

You need to know the street names of the drugs that could be offered to your children. Explain the hazards and effects of drug and alcohol use, including smoking. Discuss how drugs and alcohol will increase their vulnerability, reduce their control, and diminish their judgment, thereby putting them at extreme risk. Reinforce the message that you are there for backup in any situation where the irresponsible behavior of their friends jeopardizes their safety.

Get a commitment from your children that they will not drink and drive nor will they get in a car if anyone else who will drive is "under the influence." **Your children should either be transported by sober drivers, be able to call you up at any time and from anywhere and have you pick them up, or carry enough money to take a taxi home.**

If teens are part of a responsible crowd, they should be encouraged to have "designated drivers" on a rotational basis who abstain from drinking. Better yet, encourage your children's involvement with church or synagogue teen groups, sports, or other community activities that provide social events that are non-alcoholic. For traditional events such as senior proms, join with other parents to work out arrangements that will keep participants safe.

Be on the alert for teen parties, or if your children have a regular group that they hang out with. These are the most likely situations for underage drinking and drug use. Peer pressure and wanting to be part of the crowd often push children into excess. Check with the host parent of any teen get-together to ensure that the activities will be monitored and that you are in agreement on what is permissible.

Never allow a teen party in your home when you are not there. Not only could this contribute to unsupervised trouble, but you can be held liable for anything that occurs on your property. Do not allow your teens to attend parties elsewhere if there is no adult supervision.

It helps to be a role model for your children if you expect them to resist the pressure to smoke, drink, or use drugs. Set an example of healthy ways to relax and enjoy yourself through regular exercise, constructive pursuits, and an appreciation for personal wellness.

For children to refuse their peers and feel comfortable saying "no," they need to see adults pursuing other alternatives. If you make positive lifestyle choices yourself, your children are more likely to follow suit. They can more easily make the right choices if they know that the support and commitment already exists in their home environment.

You also need to be prepared to take action at the first sign that your child has a drinking or drug problem. Plan on intervention in a way that clearly communicates your disapproval, concern, and commitment to get your children the help they need. You and your child must acknowledge that the problem exists before recovery can begin. Talk to a social worker or substance abuse counselor to discuss drug treatment strategies. Your child may benefit from joining a support group and/or treatment program.

If the crowd your child is a part of exhibits the same self-destructive behavior, you will need to separate your child from the negative influences of these particular peers. If the school your child attends is a hotbed of substance abuse, you can lobby to have your child moved to another school or you might want to consider a private placement in a more structured environment if you can afford it.

Social Pressures and Sex

Teen pregnancy, sexually transmitted diseases, and date rape are the reality for more adolescents than ever before, and at earlier ages. Kids are driven to a false sophistication before they have the emotional maturity to deal with relationships. They are the victims of Hollywood hype—with a distorted view of sex.

Many teens are becoming sexually active at young ages. Moreover, it is not "safe sex," not for their physical well-being or their emotional development. In the midst of all this sexual hyperactivity is real confusion. These kids are out there "doing it," but they do not really know what they are doing and they do not think about the serious consequences.

Just as you have to be prepared to address substance abuse issues head-on, you need to be out front on human sexuality. This subject can be decidedly uncomfortable for parents to discuss with their children. However, if you do not, someone else will, and it might not be the kind of information or experience that you want your child to have.

You cannot count on the schools to give your children comprehensive sex education. Even if they do, it might come too late. Kids are having sex and they are getting hurt, often because of their own carelessness and the inability of youth to focus on consequences. AIDS is increasing most dramatically in the teen and young adult population. The U.S. teen pregnancy rates are among the highest of developed nations.

Many younger girls are coerced into sex when they really do not want it. If a girl is smitten with a boy, she may feel this is the way to keep him. Or she might be dating an older guy who is more experienced and more insistent. Sometimes a boy will push for sex and the girl is not effective in resisting—she does not clearly communicate, "No, and I mean it."

Boys need to be taught that "scoring" with an unwilling partner is rape. In one study of middle and high school boys, a high percentage said they expected sexual favors if they spent money ($10) on a date. Have your daughters pay their own way or they might come up against this attitude.

Unfortunately, many schools are not teaching a course in real world relationships, mutual respect, and effective communications between the sexes. That is why parents need to explore these issues with their children. Children will not figure these things out by themselves except through trial and error, and the playing field today is just too dangerous to allow that. You need to discuss sexual issues in an age-appropriate way throughout your child's development.

When your children are young, it is enough that they know the correct names for the parts of their anatomies. They also need to understand at an early age that they have ownership of their body and personal rights. As they get older and want to know more, help them to appreciate both the emotional and physical differences and similarities between boys and girls.

Your children need to be comfortable in discussing emerging curiosity with an understanding parent. If all of these factors are in place before puberty, then the stage is set to positively deal with raging hormones, misinformation, and peer pressure when they reach adolescence.

It is important to prepare yourself for the likely questions they will ask you. Figure out ahead of time what you will say about teen sex, sex before marriage, oral sex, and other issues that could come up. That way you will not stumble over an answer or be embarrassed.

Help your child delay the first sexual experience until an age and circumstance when it makes sense and will not harm the personal psyche or be damaging in other ways. Steer your children into constructive pursuits. Set clear curfew limits. Know their companions and their whereabouts. Practice typical scenarios with them and how to effectively resist pressure for early sex. Reinforce the need for safe and protective measures in sexual involvements. You can help your children to understand their responsibilities for mature and healthy relationships in their lives.

Alert your children to the possibilities of sexual harassment by adults or their peers either at school, a part-time job, or while babysitting. They should be prepared to clearly set limits if anyone makes unwanted sexual overtures. Tell them to report the behavior to you and you will help them deal with it and avoid further contact with an offender.

Campus Safety

Do you think that coming up with the tuition money is the biggest obstacle to a college education? Once you get a child into an institution of higher learning, the item most likely to interfere with an education is alcohol abuse. It is the single most serious hazard to the physical health and emotional well-being of students.

Drunken students disrupt the sleep and study time of their peers and physically attack other students as well as destroy property. Alcohol is involved in the majority of rapes and almost all violent incidents on campus.

As a parent, you have a double challenge. You need to encourage your own children to abstain from or carefully control alcohol consumption, and you have to teach them self-protective measures so they do not become victims at the hands of fellow students who are binge drinkers.

If a college roommate is a problem, the student must be prepared to complain and demand a new roommate or to be moved. The parent must be prepared to stand behind this demand with school officials.

Colleges and universities are plagued by the same problems with crime as the rest of society. Some crimes are committed by students, some by college workers, and others by clever criminals who can blend with the environment and take advantage of lax security and the careless behavior of youths that makes them easy targets.

Parents may have a false sense that these institutions of higher learning are the guardians of their children who are out on their own for the first time. The reality of college crime shows otherwise, but institutions do not advertise the seriousness of the problem for fear they would lose enrollment.

Most places fail to acknowledge the prevalence of crime. As a result, they do not sufficiently educate the students on crime awareness and prevention. College administrators are not the only ones who fail to live up to their responsibilities in this area. Students often ignore safety rules on campus, such as propping open residence doors, or they abandon their common sense in the face of new freedoms. They may "party" with people they do not know well and behave in irresponsible and dangerous ways. The consequences can be, and often are, tragic.

Much of this crime can be prevented through some simple precautions. Find out as much as you can about a particular institution and its crime history. If the college will not disclose this information or brushes you off with some general statement that is designed to reassure you while withholding any specifics, talk to the local police.

Ask about the types of crimes committed on and around campus and their frequency. Discuss where safe and unsafe areas are on campus, or where certain locations in close proximity of the college are that are high-crime areas. It makes sense to avoid these areas.

You also want to obtain specifics on the type of security measures in place on campus as well as policies and rules about safe practices. Check if the school provides specific information to students about security issues on campus, off-campus housing concerns, and crime prevention approaches.

Ask for a copy of any materials handed out to orient students, and check with the college newspaper editor for an opinion on how forthcoming the administration is about campus crime. Does the college newspaper report the details of crimes on campus or against students as they occur? Is there some other mechanism to alert students about specific crimes and trends in criminal activity?

Try to instill good safety habits in your children before they go off to college, but reinforce your concern for them in this new situation. It is important to transfer the advice presented in this book to the college environment. You can give a copy of this book as a going-away present to new college students.

Highlight the need to lock doors and windows, travel in groups, avoid isolated areas, especially at night, and stay aware of their surroundings. In addition to behaving in a safety-conscious way, students need to provide a neighborhood watch of sorts for each other, reporting suspicious activities or persons to campus security and local police.

Key Points To Remember

- Alcohol and drugs are the greatest threat to teen safety.
- Firearm homicide is the second leading cause of death for teens.
- Adolescents are twice as likely as adults to be the victims of violent crime.
- Many adolescents suffer psychological trauma from their exposure to violence.
- Positive relationships with parents can help adolescents resist threats to their health.
- Community activities can offer youths an outlet and a way to contribute to society.
- There are millions of latchkey kids ages 5-13 left on their own each day.
- Unsupervised children can get lonely and afraid, and they are more likely to be victimized or get into trouble.
- After-school programs or arrangements with other people for adult support are preferable to leaving a child alone.

- Have children check in with you or a neighbor when they get home from school. Keep important numbers posted by the phone.
- Go over basic safety rules for on the street and in the home.
- Discuss telephone techniques and ways to screen visitors.
- If your children are responsible for themselves while at home, agree on family policies, allowable activities, and instructions they are expected to follow.
- Adolescents are in jeopardy at most schools. They are at highest risk when they are isolated and out of the classroom.
- Encourage your children to recognize danger signs and avoid trouble.
- Discuss their concerns and the reality of their school experience and help them develop effective ways to cope.
- Support conflict resolution and mediation training and programs in the school; these have been shown to reduce violence and improve the learning environment.
- Your teens should never drink and drive or get into a vehicle where the driver is under the influence of alcohol or drugs.
- Do not allow your children at unsupervised parties where drinking will occur.
- React quickly and decisively if you think your child has a drinking or drug abuse problem.
- Adolescents are sexually active, with transmission of AIDS on the increase and high teen pregnancy rates. Date rape is also a major problem.
- Discuss human sexuality and responsible behavior in an age-appropriate way with your children as they develop. Help them to deal with peer pressure.

- College drinking is the greatest threat to your child's education and safety.
- Evaluate the security of the college campus and surrounding area, and encourage your children to adopt safety awareness and take precautions to protect themselves.

Practice Scenarios

What if... ?

Your 8th grade friends offer you marijuana when you go camping in the woods.

Someone is trying to break into your house, and your parents are at work.

Your 16-year-old boyfriend is pressuring you for "real sex" because he wants you to prove you love him; if you do not have intercourse with him, some other girl will.

A bigger kid at school pushes you and tells you to give him your lunch money.

Two boys you know are going to settle an argument at the ball field after school, and one of them has a gun.

You are at a great party, but everyone is drinking, including the guy that drove you to the party.

Your roommate at college parties all the time and is careless about locking the dorm room door.

13

Defending Yourself

Tricia returned from work and stood by the mailboxes of her apartment complex going through her letters. She did not hear the man approach from behind in tennis shoes because she was engrossed in her mail. The next thing she knew, he had his arm locked around her neck and he was dragging her backwards toward the laundry room. She froze for a minute, but then she got angry as she realized what was happening, and the adrenaline started flowing. She turned her head to the side, bit him hard in his arm and then shoved her elbow fast and sharp into her assailant's midsection. As he loosened his grip, she stomped the heel of her pump full force on his foot, and then charged out the building into the front courtyard screaming as loud as she could, "I'm being attacked. Call the police." The "police" happened to be a neighbor just returning from duty. When he rushed into the building, he saw the "assailant" slumped against the wall, holding his foot and his stomach, obviously in pain.

Myths and Realities

Are women really able to defend themselves effectively? Answer that question with a resounding "Yes!" Any other attitude or belief puts you in the mindset of a victim. You are conquered at the outset, conceding defeat before the attack has begun. Predatory criminals count on women feeling helpless; they do not expect resistance.

Of course, the goal is to avoid confrontation in the first place. Despite your best efforts at awareness and prevention, you still may be targeted for crime. If this happens, you need to understand that you can effectively deal with it and maintain your composure in spite of threatening circumstances.

Verbal self-defense skills can help you to change the balance of power in an attack situation. For starters, you can warn off an attacker to keep his distance and leave you alone, or you can scream to get the attention of others. Either of those approaches might be enough to deter an attack.

You might also be able to negotiate with your assailant, stall for time, or distract him long enough to get away. It is possible to put a criminal at ease, give him a false sense of security, convince him that you are not a threat, and generally manipulate him to drop his guard and give you the chance to escape.

Your first and foremost concern should be getting away from your assailant. Where property is concerned, give it up. But if you are still under attack and it is evident that your attacker wants you, you have to be ready to defend yourself and flee.

If you are ever being beaten and cannot or will not defend yourself, you need to minimize the damage to your body. Lie on the ground with your knees tucked up against your stomach and cover your head with your arms. You will be less seriously hurt than if you give your attacker full access to your body.

In an attack situation, always consider what is available to you to use in your defense and how you can hurt your attacker enough so that you can escape. It helps to get him off balance or use the element of surprise to thwart an attack. Keep assessing your situation and what options are available to you. If one strategy does not work, try another.

Every attack situation is different. Only you can assess your assailant and decide what is the best method of self-defense for you and the most likely ways to gain some control and avoid bodily harm. You need to understand your options and determine which tactics and techniques will work for you—as well as your readiness to use them.

If you decide to fight back, marshall your forces and give it all you have to incapacitate your assailant. Then get out of there fast. **Never lose sight that the goal is escape.** Always run to an open and occupied area, and scream that you are being attacked. Do not head for a deserted area or alley in a panic where you might be recaptured and there are no other people to help you.

If, on the other hand, your assailant is the one to flee, never go after him, no matter how angry the attack may have made you and even if he has your favorite purse in hand. Save the energy for reporting the crime to the police and giving a good description.

Laws and Liabilities

According to our legal system, you have the right to defend yourself. However, high crime rates aside, human life is considered more important than personal property under the law. That means you cannot shoot a burglar for stealing your jewelry.

Even when you are in immediate and imminent danger, you can only use "reasonable and necessary force" to defend yourself. You can be charged with and found guilty of assault with a deadly weapon if you had one and used it against an assailant who did not have a weapon.

If you use a weapon to defend yourself, you will be dealing with the criminal justice system. Your weapon will be confiscated and you will need a lawyer to represent you. You may very well end up with criminal and civil charges filed against you.

As unbelievable as it may seem, criminals have successfully sued and won settlements from their victims. It helps to understand the legal context when you are tempted to rush out and buy a handgun for self-protection.

If you feel that you absolutely must have a weapon, apply for any required licenses or permits, and make sure you understand the legal consequences of carrying it and using it. Make sure you get the necessary training to know how to operate the weapon, to safely carry or store it, and to effectively use it. Keep in mind that the discharge of a gun can hurt innocent people and a stolen weapon will most likely be used in the commission of a crime.

In most states, it is legal to carry a defensive spray. Although these sprays can stop an attacker, they are non-lethal. They will not permanently disable or kill the assailant. These are particularly popular with women in urban areas. However, some states have restrictions or may require licensing. Check with local police on what is required in your jurisdiction for defensive sprays and other weapons.

Carrying chemical weapons onto a commercial flight is a federal offense. If you travel by air and want to take a spray canister with you, you need to pack it in your checked luggage. It will be confiscated by airport officials if you try to transport it in your purse or carry-on luggage.

Pros and Cons of Weapons

In most cases, a weapon will not do you any good, and it can cause you great harm. You have to be trained to use it effectively. You have to practice to stay proficient. You have to prevent it from being taken from you and used against you. Your having a weapon is more likely to increase the danger to you and your loved ones than it is to protect you from a criminal.

Many criminals carry weapons to increase their own courage and intimidate their victims into compliance. When you both have weapons, it raises the stakes, and a violent confrontation is more likely. If you have a weapon, you have to be prepared to kill another human being with it and suffer the emotional and legal consequences of that act.

America has more guns than any other country; it also has more murders using those guns. A little more than half of those murders are perpetrated by one stranger against another. However, it is a sad fact that many domestic disagreements end in homicide just because a gun was available when tempers flared.

According to the Bureau of Alcohol, Tobacco and Firearms, Americans own over 200 million guns, and about a third of those are handguns. Each day, about 1.2 million latchkey children return to homes where there is a gun, and children are often the victims of accidental gun shootings. In addition, a majority of children with guns in the school say they are getting them from their parents' homes.

To sum it up, a handgun kept in the house is far more likely to cause serious injury or death to a family member than an intruder. It is also more likely to be stolen by a burglar than to be used to defend against one.

You might find that when it comes right down to it, you will hesitate to use it in your defense, and it could be taken from you and used against you, instead. Unless you are a crack shot, with nerves of steel, and lots of practice in real world situations—and you know that you could shoot to kill—forget a gun.

However, if you do have a firearm in your home, keep it locked and out of the curious access of children. You should never go investigating—gun in hand—if you hear an intruder. Lock yourself and your family in your "safe" room, call the police, and take cover behind a solid object, like the far side of the bed. Bullets can go through wooden bedroom doors and wallboard.

If the intruder comes to the door, yell loudly, "I am armed, in fear of my life, and if you enter this room I will shoot you." This statement not only warns him off, it establishes your basis for self-defense. If he still keeps coming after being warned, then you can assume he means you bodily harm and you would be justified in defending yourself even if that involves using a gun as a last resort.

Knives can be effective self-defense weapons if you have lots of practice and skill and you never let your assailant know you have one until you strike. The best knife for this purpose has a 4-6 inch blade with a bowie-style point, a cross guard to protect your hand, a grip of hard rubber or leather, and a deep enough sheath to carry it in. Folding knives are handy, but they will slow down your reaction time and it is hard to secretly open one for action.

Again, as with a gun, this weapon can be taken from you and used against you. You also need to have the skill and the will to use it against an assailant. Check with your jurisdiction on what type of knives are considered concealed weapons. In the home, you need to keep a knife out of the reach of children. You also have to consider where you will have it so you can gain access if you are attacked in your home.

Some women, who did not have knives for self-defense purposes, have effectively incapacitated assailants with other sharp objects found in their homes. First they put their assailants off guard by pretending to cooperate. Then they defended themselves with surprise strikes at their captors using carving knives, large scissors, or screw drivers.

Other Devices

There are several other devices on the market that are promoted as "personal safety" aids. Some of these may qualify as "concealed weapons" and you still might have to worry about liability issues and assault charges if an innocent person is injured or you use "excessive force."

The devices have varying degrees of effectiveness depending on circumstances. As in the case of guns and knives, you also have to be willing to use them. They do not take the place of awareness and personal preparedness, but there are situations where they might be useful.

Women can obtain different types of noisemakers. They cannot stop a determined criminal, but they are all designed to call attention and may help ward off an attack. One type is a police whistle. A woman has to have the presence of mind to use it, there has to be someone to hear it who is motivated enough to get her help, and it may annoy an attacker.

A better choice is a personal alarm. Several on the market have different sounds—shrieking, sirens, and horns—and some also have a "strobe" light. One company, Quorum International (602-780-5533), has a wide range of personal protection products, including an affordable personal attack alarm the size of a pager that features state-of-the-art technology. This also could be a good item to equip your children with to call attention to themselves if they feel they are in jeopardy.

A multi-use item to have for the car that provides both light and protection is a police flashlight. By directing the beam at the face of anyone approaching you, you effectively set up a light shield where you can see the person, but the person cannot see you. It can also be used as an effective self-defense weapon because of its length and heft, something like swinging a lead pipe at your assailant.

If you want to consider stick protection, a 5-1/2 inch baton called the Kubotan can inflict significant pain on an attacker. Effective use takes training and practice and you have to get up close to your attacker to use it. It was invented by a martial artist by the same name. If the idea of wielding a short stick for self-protection appeals to you, you can call the company toll-free that manufactures the device under the name

Persuader (800-PR24-USA) and find out about training near you.

Another type of device is the stun gun. Electric stunners are fairly effective in bringing down an attacker. You have to make good contact with the prongs against the skin of the assailant, through clothes, somewhere in his midsection. It might not work if your assailant is wearing heavy clothes or leather. You also need to maintain contact for about five seconds to incapacitate your assailant. Obviously, close physical contact is needed to do this effectively, and if you can touch him, he can grab you.

A longer range device, called the Air Taser, can be used as a conventional stun gun or to launch probes attached to 15 feet of wire into the clothes of your attacker. Powerful electronic impulses supposedly jam the neural system of an assailant so that he loses control of his body for a few minutes. The unit is about the size of a flashlight and it is powered by a 9-volt battery.

There is real competition in the personal protection device field among companies producing defensive sprays. Chemical sprays, including tear gas, cause profuse tearing, choking, and an extreme burning sensation. Tear gas will not stop an assailant who is drunk, high on drugs, or mentally agitated, and it will not stop vicious dogs.

Pepper spray temporarily blinds an attacker when you spray it in his face from 4 to 6 feet away, causes extreme pain, and makes breathing difficult. It can stop a charging animal and it works on people who are drunk or on drugs. Buy a canister that contains at least 10 percent oleoresin capsium with a minimum 10 seconds worth of spray.

Some sprays contain both agents, and the effect can last about 20 minutes. However, the spray may not always work immediately. Also, if your attacker wears glasses, that may provide enough eye protection to offset the effects of the spray.

You should practice using a spray, use it correctly, and check periodically on expiration dates. If you are going to carry a spray, carry it in your hand so it is immediately ready, not in a purse or somewhere else where you will have to get it out. You might want to also keep a unit in your car and your home near your bedside in a concealed location but within easy reach. Again, keep these units out of the hands of children.

When walking to and from locations, conceal the canister in your hand in a ready-to-use position but with the nozzle pointed to the ground. Warn your assailant off. Tell him to go away and leave you alone. Do not forewarn him that you have the defensive spray, though, or challenge him by holding it out as if you are going to spray.

If he keeps approaching, start spraying and then point the spray at your assailant's face, rather than pointing and then spraying. That way you will know that the unit is working properly and can aim the actual spray better. If you depress the release button with your thumb and cannot feel any spray with your index finger, you will know it is not working, but your assailant will not be any the wiser.

If you are outdoors when it is windy, the spray could come back at you, so it would not make sense to aim the canister at your attacker. However, you could spray your fingers and rub them in the attacker's eyes if you could not ward him off with verbal self-defense.

Martial Arts

Knowing that you can physically defend yourself if need be can actually reduce the chance that you will ever have to, so this is an area that deserves serious consideration. It takes some time and commitment, but a woman does not have to be strong, agile, or coordinated to learn.

Physical defense techniques are difficult to learn from a book, although one of the many excellent books written on the topic from the female perspective can give you a good overview of the available approaches or help reinforce what you learn in a course. There are also some videos on the market that are geared toward demonstrating self-defense techniques to women.

However, the best way to learn is by doing under the tutelage of a qualified instructor. It takes practice to build confidence and skill. Also, learning to judge when to use a particular technique is as important as knowing how to do it.

If you are in for the long haul, you can commit to one of the many martial arts programs that are taught as a mastery sport over several years. Otherwise, you should look for a women's survival arts class that may borrow techniques from one or several disciplines to teach you physical self defense. Courses are available across the country through private businesses, non-profit organizations, educational institutions, and community-sponsored activities.

The best programs incorporate class discussions on attitude and awareness and should give you the chance to practice your responses in simulated attacks. One self-defense training program for women, called IMPACT, is available in most major American cities. For more information, call 800-345-5425.

Enrolling in and completing this type of program can have a transforming effect on a woman. For one thing, it helps her to face her fears and come away with a sense of empowerment—that she can be her own protector in an uncertain world. Young girls do not grow up punching each other out in the ball field like boys do. For many women, a self-defense class is the first time in their lives that they actually hit someone.

This type of training can help women to visualize fighting back, if necessary, and this can be a psychological boost to self-esteem. Learning that you can meet physical force with skill and deflect an attack can be a liberating experience. It goes a long way toward overcoming the sense of helplessness that mark many women as victims.

All of the martial arts rely on the concepts of balance and self-discipline. By being involved in this kind of training, a woman learns to focus her mind, body, and emotions for greater alertness and control. This not only serves her well in threatening situations, it can enhance many other aspects of her life as well.

The goals of these courses are the same as the goals of this book: teaching women to be responsible for their actions and reactions, and showing them how to stay aware and prepared. Mentally and physically rehearsing possible confrontations fosters good decision-making skills and quick, effective responses.

If All Else Fails

If you find yourself in a life-threatening situation, one thing that will help you tremendously is to breathe evenly. This will give you a sense of being centered and grounded. Most people, when met with a fearful situation, breathe fast and shallow. If you breathe deeply and slowly, it will help you relax.

Practice this technique whenever you find yourself in a stressful situation in your everyday activities and it will become second nature to you. If you panic, you will not be able to think straight, and keeping your wits about you is crucial to survival.

You would not normally resort to physical defense or choose to fight back unless you are in imminent danger. That is why the first critical steps in determining any course of action are to **assess how dangerous your situation is and the intent of your assailant.** However, there are three situations in which you are better off fighting back immediately, because it may be your only chance:

- If someone is attempting to kill you (knife, gun, strangulation).
- If someone is going to abduct you and take you to a more secluded place.

- If someone is going to physically restrain you with rope, handcuffs, or duct tape.

In the first situation, you have nothing to lose. You are fighting for your life. In the second and third situations, you are in a much stronger position initially to defend yourself and flee than you will be subsequently. Chances are that once your assailant has you isolated or completely in his power the violence will escalate.

Since you probably will not be able to match the strength of your opponent head-on, do not try to. That is a mistake that many women with no training in self-defense make. If someone grabs your wrist, pulling straight back means you are in a tug of war. However, if you move your hand sideways through your assailant's thumb and index finger, you might break the grip.

If someone grabs you from behind in an arm lock around your neck, trying to pull his arm away is futile. However, turning your head to the right may take the pressure off your windpipe. Since you will not be fighting for breath, you can reach for your assailant's pinky and bend it back as hard and as fast as you can to get him to release you.

The sooner you get away, the less likely you are to be injured, dragged off, or forced to the ground. If you end up on the ground, you can use your leg for kicking power. You may be able to bend your knee and kick up and out at the shin, kneecap, or groin area. If your assailant has you pinned, you will need to pretend cooperation until you are in a position to fight back.

There are two techniques that can be used in a sexual assault to disable a man when you have first disarmed him by pretending to go along. You have to be convincing enough in your compliance to get positioned for either action and then have the resolve to follow through. Either action on your part can put your assailant in shock and give you the chance to escape.

If you need your courage bolstered, consider that most rapists have a capacity for incredible violence, and many brutalize or murder their victims after the rape is completed. You can also think about all the people you love who will be hurt by your rape or murder if you do not take action to protect yourself.

One technique is to gently stroke the scrotum of your attacker. This will relax him and he will not expect your next move. Using both hands, grab his testes and squeeze as hard as you can while pulling them away from the body in a sudden jerk.

The other technique is to caress your attacker's face, with your fingertips resting gently on his temples. Then push your thumbs into his eyeballs with sudden and swift pressure as hard as you can.

You can back out on either of these techniques at the last moment without your assailant knowing your intentions. While you may or may not be able to go through with these techniques, keep them in the back of your mind. Remember, the choice is between you inflicting harm or having harm inflicted on you. You will have to decide what to do.

If someone is shooting at you, reduce your exposure and move out of the line of fire. Turn sideways, drop low to the ground, seek solid cover. If you are going to run away, stay low and move in a zig-zag pattern. Present a moving and erratic target.

If someone comes at you with a knife, try to stay out of striking distance. Use anything at your disposal as a shield, such as a purse or briefcase. If you have an umbrella or cane, that can be struck against the hand of the assailant holding the knife. Wrap your hand and arm with something protective—a belt, jacket, or newspaper so that you can ward off the knife with less likelihood of slashing while you try to disarm or escape your attacker.

Strike Zones

Despite a woman's disadvantage in size and strength, she can hurt an attacker enough to get away by learning a few effective ways to hit an assailant in vulnerable areas of the body. There are 10 striking areas (Figure 6) where you can inflict severe pain. These areas are:

1. Temples
2. Eyes
3. Bridge of Nose
4. Chin
5. Windpipe
6. Solar Plexus
7. Groin
8. Knees (front or sides)
9. Shins
10. Insteps (top of foot)

You also should consider what you have at hand that can be used as weapons, for instance, your keys or an open ballpoint pen. If you hold a pen in your strong hand with the thumb over the top for reinforcement and jam it down into a soft area of your attacker's body, you can create an extremely painful puncture wound.

Your own body is a natural weapon as well. You can butt with your head, strike with your elbow or knee, kick or stomp with your heel, thrust with your fingers, or use a heel of the palm blow that is very effective. Just remember, **look at your target and strike or stomp through it.** For example, imagine a palm blow going through your assailant's head rather than stopping at the bridge of his nose. Exhale while you deliver the blow. You will deliver a more powerful and effective blow that way.

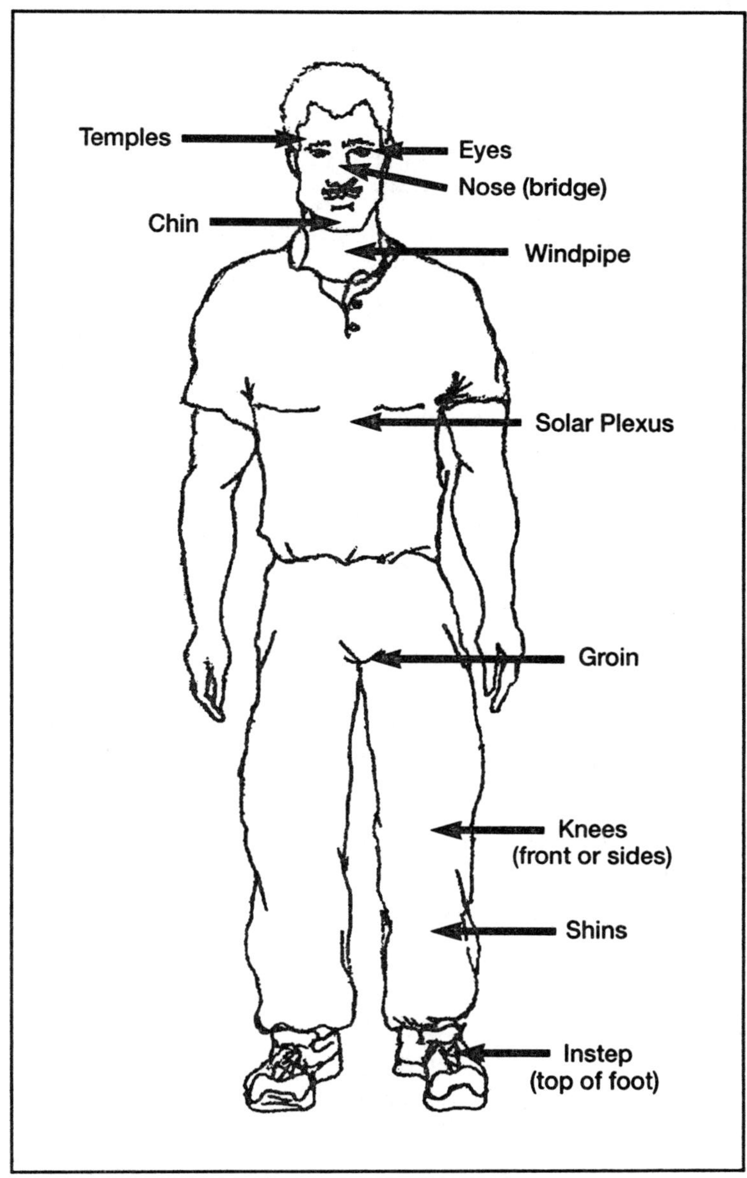

Figure 6. Striking areas of the body for self-defense

If women are going to replace a sense of helplessness with one of competence, they need to understand and be prepared to use methods of self-defense to protect themselves when necessary.

Once you are in a confrontation, use your skills of observation and manipulation to determine a weakness in your assailant or an object in your environment that you can use to distract, deflect, or defend with. Tap into your survival instinct, too, so you will not let your abhorrence of violence get in the way of defending yourself.

Most women who are mothers would defend their children to the death. Be a mother to yourself when you are under attack and call up that fierceness to get yourself out of a dangerous situation. Remember your right to life, liberty, and the pursuit of happiness. This person, who is accosting you, is trying to take those away from you and those you love.

If you decide to defend yourself, do it swiftly, with every bit of effort at your command. Follow through completely. If you are mentally prepared to stop an assailant, you will greatly increase your chances of success.

Most important, trust your instincts in assessing a situation and responding to it. This is one time when the highly developed sixth sense of women comes in handy. You have to believe in it and let it guide you. Many women have intuitions about crime occurring shortly before it does, but they ignore their own internal warning system. Tune into that and you may well avoid threatening situations in the first place.

Key Points To Remember

- Women can effectively defend themselves.
- Use verbal self-defense to warn an attacker off.
- Give up property and get away, if possible.

- If under attack, assess your options.
- If you physically resist, incapacitate your assailant and escape.
- Under the law you can defend yourself, but unnecessary force makes you liable.
- Weapons can be effective for self-defense, but only if you are highly proficient in their use and willing to use them.
- Guns in the home are more dangerous to the occupants than to an intruder.
- Other protective devices, such as shriek alarms, stun guns, and chemical sprays, have varying degrees of effectiveness, depending on the circumstances.
- Learning physical defense techniques can empower a woman and boost self-esteem.
- When under attack, stay calm, center yourself, and breathe deeply.
- Try to assess your situation and the intent of the assailant.
- Stall or divert the attack if you can; defend yourself if you are in imminent danger of bodily harm.
- Trust your instincts in assessing a situation and in choosing the best way to respond to a particular set of circumstances.

Practice Scenarios

What if... ?

A man pins you up against a parked car and tells you to give him your money.

Your boyfriend is in a drunken rage as he accuses you of cheating on him and starts hurling punches at you.

You wake up in a motel room with a man holding a knife at your throat as he starts tearing at your nightgown.

The new man you are dating comes on too strong, too fast, and he is dragging you toward the bedroom where he says he keeps the handcuffs.

You come to collect your clothes from the dryer in the laundry room and a man covers your mouth with his hand and pushes you to the ground.

You go to the parking garage after class and a man gets off the elevator when you do, grabs your arm, and tells you he is taking you to his car.

14

Surviving a Crime

Peg was out at the bird feeder when she noticed the van pull into her neighbor's driveway. A man got out and rang the front doorbell several times, then he peered into the front windows. She knew no one was at home because both the husband and wife worked and their two children were in school. She watched from her protected spot at the rear of her house, expecting him to leave. Instead, another man got out and the two went around the back of the house to the deck area, out of her sight. She then heard the muffled sound of glass cracking, and that is when she rushed into her house and called 911. She reported a "crime in progress" and gave the dispatcher detailed information, including the license plate of the van that she could see with her bird-watching binoculars. Within 10 minutes, two police cars arrived and the burglars were apprehended. They were later found to be responsible for a large number of burglaries and armed robberies in that area, and the van was a stolen vehicle. Peg was written up in the local paper as the grandma who stopped a crime spree.

Reporting Suspicious Activities

Some of the biggest advantages of Neighborhood Watch programs are that the people involved look out for each other, provide an active network of backup and support, and serve as the eyes and ears of local police and sheriff departments. However, you do not have to be a member of such a program to be a concerned citizen, do your civic duty, and help combat crime by being alert and willing to report suspicious activities.

Criminals would have a harder time if law abiding citizens took an active interest in their surroundings and contacted the police on crimes in progress that they witness. Do not assume someone else will call. Do not brush off unusual or strange happenings in your area. By notifying police at the first sign of trouble, you may very well prevent a crime from occurring in your area or becoming a victim yourself.

Awareness involves looking and listening for any incidents or persons that seem out of place for the area you are in which may indicate that illegal activities are under way. Unusual noises, such as screaming, gunshots, the sound of breaking glass, or continuously barking dogs should be reported immediately to the police so they can investigate.

Always report any loitering near schools or parks. Someone hanging around could be a sex offender or drug dealer. In parking areas, someone that seems to be wandering from car to car or standing in a partially concealed area might be a car thief, mugger, or rapist. Someone waiting in front of a home or business could be planning a burglary or serving as a lookout. Someone running across property or in clothing inappropriate for jogging, may be leaving the scene of a crime. Your suspicions of burglary or robbery are naturally increased if the person is carrying any items of property. Strangers driving slowly through a neighborhood several times or sitting in a parked car should also be viewed with suspicion.

If someone pulls up to a neighbor's house in a van and starts loading items from the residence, do not assume that this is being done with the neighbor's knowledge or permission. You can call your neighbor and check. If you do not get your neighbor, you hear a recorded message, or you do not recognize the voice of the person who answers the phone, call the police and ask that they send a patrol car to check it out.

You should be on the lookout for signs of ongoing criminal activity. Heavy human traffic at a residence on a regular basis may indicate drug dealing or other illegal activity. Be suspicious of any vehicles loaded with merchandise or weapons. Continuous "repair" operations at a non-business location may be a tip-off that stolen property is being altered in some way. If property is offered to you at a very low price, these items could be stolen.

Many crimes involve vehicles. Someone trying to force entry into a car or taking off accessories or other mechanical parts is probably a car thief. A newly abandoned vehicle may have been stolen from someone else and then dumped. Always report anyone being forced to enter a car, especially if it is a woman or a child; this could be an abduction.

Report any crime you witness or any other suspicious activity as soon as possible. As more people have cellular phones in their cars, police are finding that citizens using them to alert authorities make up a "mobile posse" of sorts. More than 600,000 emergency calls are made each month throughout the country, and people report drunk drivers, drug deals, stranded motorists, carjackings, and burglaries in progress. So if you have one, it not only provides security for yourself, but also a way for you to contribute to the safety of others. Cellular phones are truly a major aid to personal protection and crime prevention.

Whenever you contact the police, be prepared to report what you have observed and the location as clearly and calmly as possible, giving as much detail as you can. It helps if you give your name, address, and phone number so the police can get back to you for additional information if needed or to ask you to serve as a witness. If you do not want to get involved, you can still report an incident anonymously as a "concerned citizen." The important thing is to make a report.

Describing a Criminal

If you watch enough television, you are bound to see a show where an artist's rendition of a person based on a description by a witness is used to develop a "composite" drawing for the police to use in investigating a crime. A good likeness is often sufficient to put out an alert and capture the suspect. In the 1995 bombing of the Federal Building in Oklahoma City, an artist's drawing helped to identify and apprehend a suspect. Law enforcement agencies also retain photo files of convicted criminals, and visual or computer matches are possible. You also might be called in to observe a "line up" through a one-way viewing window to see if you can make a positive identification of your assailant from among a group of people.

If you understand how important an accurate description can be to the law enforcement process, it might help you keep the presence of mind in a threatening situation to note details that will later help the police do their job. However, try to be observant during the commission of a crime without being obvious about it or indicating to the perpetrators that you are committing their images to memory. Better that they think you are just another victim who is too shocked to retain any information important enough for the police to track them down.

If you consider the elements now that make up a good description, you are more likely to mentally catalog these items when confronted with a crime. You can also note details as a way to focus your energy in a positive way during a frightening experience. It can give you a purpose to help fight the panic. Even if you cannot stop the crime as it is happening, you can subsequently provide information that may help law enforcement officials apprehend the criminal. At a time when you are feeling helpless or angry because you are being victimized, this can help you exercise a certain amount of control over the situation.

The more details, the better the description. However, if you do not know something or could not accurately tell, it is better to leave out an item than to give wrong information which could mislead police. Basic identifying information on a perpetrator includes: sex, age, race, height, weight, physical build, color of hair, color of eyes, and complexion. This can be expanded with additional details:

- Did your assailant have any facial hair such as a mustache or beard?
- Did he wear glasses, and if so, what did his frames look like?
- What was the style, length, and texture of his hair—long and shaggy, pony tail, crew cut, block cut, mohawk, afro, natural, slicked back, or bald?
- Did he have sideburns—straight, flared, or mutton chops?
- What was the shape of his face—round, oval, oblong, square, or triangular? Did he have a high, medium, or low forehead?
- What were the size and shape of his eyes? Were they wide apart, medium, or close set? Would you consider them recessed, hooded, slanted, or protruding?
- Did he have any distinguishing facial features? Consider his eyebrows, nose, mouth, chin, ears, scars, or moles.
- Did he have other identifying features, such as tatoos, missing finger, limp, heavy body hair, accent, speech patterns, quality of voice, mannerisms?

You should also be able to describe the color, pattern, fabric, and style of the clothing he was wearing—shirt, pants, tie, sweater, sweatsuit, socks, shoes, jacket or coat, hat, mask, head covering—and any accessories, such as jewelry, fanny pack, or bag. If he had a weapon, what kind? Provide a description of the size, color, type, and any other unique features that you recall. If he was not wearing gloves and you noted that he touched anything with his hands, tell that to the police as well so they can lift fingerprints.

If a vehicle was used, try to provide a description of that as well—the make, model, body type, approximate year, color, any special ornaments or features, bumper stickers or decals, and any identifying dents or scratches. What was the direction that the vehicle was going in or, if used for a getaway, the route of escape? How many people were in the car? Whenever possible, get the license plate number and state. Even a partial license plate number can be traced and matched against a description of the vehicle through a computer database that can process various pieces of vehicle information and provide leads to law enforcement officials investigating crimes.

Evidence and Police Procedures

If you report a crime or incident, you should get basic information and record it so that you can track the case as it progresses through the investigative process and later the courts, if the case comes to trial. This includes the date and time that you notified police, the time the police officer arrived on the scene, the name of the law enforcement officer taking the report, the precinct or department, the report number, and procedures for obtaining a copy of the report. You also want to know the name, address, and phone number of a contact for checking on progress into the investigation of the crime.

The dignity of the victim has been damaged by the crime; the victim should not be further insulted by the investigating process. Police departments have improved on sensitivity training, but officers deal with a variety of crimes every day, and they may be understaffed and overloaded. Nonetheless, the victim needs to be treated with respect. If you are helping that person, or if you are the victim, you should insist on courtesy from those involved in the investigation. If the victim is to contribute to resolving a case, then reporting and investigative procedures need to be explained. It helps the victim understand the reasons for exhaustive questioning, physical tests, or other types of evidence gathering. If that information is not offered, ask for it. If you are dissatisfied with the responding officer, contact the supervisor.

Courts and Victimization Laws

Victims and witnesses can benefit from help in dealing with the criminal justice system during prosecution of a case. The paperwork and the process can be bewildering and it may seem like the criminal has more rights than the victim. A victim advocate—either a trained volunteer, a family member, or a friend—can help the victim stay informed about proceedings and can accompany the victim to court. Pre-trial hearings may be especially stressful because this may be the first time that the victim has to see the perpetrator since the commission of the crime. An advocate can be persistent in ensuring that an experienced prosecutor gets the case, that it is well-prepared, and that victims and witnesses are protected from intimidation by defendants. If you are not satisfied with the job being done, contact the District Attorney.

There are legislated rights for the victims of crime in all 50 states, although they vary. However, the criminal justice system today is much more enlightened about the needs and rights of victims than it was in the early 1970s when the movement for victims' rights began. These laws generally ensure that the victims are effectively represented and involved in key stages of the case, that they are provided a range of support services, and that they are compensated for medical costs and lost earnings. States with victim compensation programs are also assisted through federal grants under the 1984 Federal Victims of Crime Act.

Payments are made to people who are injured as a direct result of crime. In many cases, this includes "good samaritans" who attempted to stop a crime or catch the perpetrator. Payment for burial and related expenses can be made to the survivors of a homicide victim. These laws apply to reported crimes, and awards can be made whether or not the perpetrator is captured or convicted.

Although property loss is not usually covered under compensation laws, some states have restitution programs where part of the sentencing for convicted criminals includes repaying the victim for crime-related losses, and this may involve property damage. Many states preclude criminals from personally profiting from the publicizing of their crimes. Any money earned goes to cover the victim's expenses or may be put in a general victim compensation fund.

Other important aspects of victims' rights is the notification of progress on the case and the ability of the victim to participate in sentencing and parole decisions. The victim is notified of major decision points during the trial and sentencing process, as well as parole, release, or escape of the perpetrator. This includes a victim impact statement that describes the effects—financial, emotional, physical—that the crime has had on the victim. A victim may be able to comment on proposed sentences or later testify at a parole hearing. Victims can find out more about their rights in their states by contacting the organizations listed at the end of this chapter.

Coping with Crisis

Any type of crime—a mugging, burglary, carjacking, or sexual assault—creates problems for the victim. There is financial loss. There may be physical injury. There are serious emotional effects. The victim feels violated and the sense of security and control is shattered. Life has been disrupted in a significant way. Both the victims themselves and the witnesses to violent crimes can experience severe trauma. The same is true for family members.

The most effective ways to cope with this type of crisis involve first recognizing the reactions to trauma for what they are and understanding that there are stages to the recovery process. Although there is no way to protect a victim from experiencing these reactions, there are ways to ease the pain and promote and support the healing process. Friends and family can provide sensitivity and intervene in helpful ways to obtain resources for victim assistance. There are also things that victims can do for themselves to help regain a sense of balance and empowerment.

There are normal stages that victims have to work through in reconstructing their lives and recovering from their experiences. Depending on the nature and severity of the crime and the personality of the victim, as well as the type of support provided to the victim, these phases will be worked through at different speeds. Counseling almost invariably helps because it gives the victim an opportunity to express feelings and examine options. It can also be critical if a victim seems to be consumed by anger or fear, constantly relives the horror of the crime, or becomes depressed and suicidal.

The initial stage is shock and denial. How could this have happened to me? Or a person may suppress the incident and try to pretend it did not happen or it did not have an effect. But it did happen and it did have an effect and the victim will need to come to terms with this in order to progress down the road to recovery. That is why the denial of sexual abuse can produce such long-term damage to the victim's psyche and relationships. You have to acknowledge and address the crime in order to rebuild your life.

Being a victim of crime can evoke powerful emotions—fear, anger, guilt, shame, powerlessness, self-pity, frustration, anxiety, sadness, and grief. Not everyone will feel all of these and they may not come in a predictable order, but it is important to understand that these feelings are normal. That way, they are neither unexpected nor overwhelming when experienced. Acknowledging this roller coaster of emotion can also help friends and family members respond in appropriate and caring ways to the victim who is experiencing mood swings or who lashes out or retreats for no apparent reason.

A constellation of physical reactions may also occur following a crime. The victim may experience overwhelming fatigue and exhaustion. Sleep disturbances—either nightmares or insomnia—are not uncommon. The onset of new health problems, such as severe headaches or digestive problems, may indicate a physical reaction to the post-traumatic stress of being a crime victim. The activity level may change dramatically—a person may become immobilized and "drop out" from normal pursuits or suddenly become hyperactive, busily charging around just to have "something to do." A person's cognitive powers may falter—the victim may experience memory disturbances or have difficulty concentrating, solving problems, or making decisions.

All of this can be extremely distressing to victims and confusing to the people around them. Personal relationships and employment may be affected. Open communication and a discussion of the crime and the aftermath are important components to the coping process and are critical to long-term recovery. Sharing information helps to alleviate the isolation that most crime victims feel. It also helps sensitize those people who care about the victim and interact with the victim on a regular basis. Others have to be willing to give support to crime victims. The victims have to be able to receive this support and use the help of others as a foundation for helping themselves and surviving the crisis.

Helping Others

Just as many people are stunned by crime when they become the victim, families and friends may not know the best ways to help the victim deal with the crime. Expressing care and concern and telling the victim that you will provide ongoing support over the long haul are important first steps. If a crime has just been committed or you are the first person contacted by the victim after a crime occurs, you need to be calm and reassuring and assess the victim's need for immediate medical attention. The victim will most likely be distraught and confused and in need of your compassion and stability.

Help the victim be comfortable about discussing the crime. Say, "I am sorry that this happened to you. Can you tell me about it?" Some people may not want to talk about the experience. Others may want to repeat the details over and over. Listen and reassure. Let the victim express emotions. Do not make judgments and **never blame the victim, whatever the circumstances.**

It is important to get the message across to the victim, "It wasn't your fault." This is not the time to imply that the victim's behavior or lack of awareness were in some way responsible. The victim will do enough self-blaming without your help. You need to discourage this process, not reinforce it. This is also not the time for making trite statements about why something happened or that the victim "will get over it in time." A person's life is never the same after a crime as it was before. However, the victim can regain control and find the strength to move beyond the crime in a productive way.

When children are the victims of crime, they will also suffer emotional trauma, but adults should not assume that they know how intensely the children are affected by the experience. Something that seems like a minor theft may be especially disturbing to your child. On the other hand, in a situation such as child molestation, you might be more emotionally devastated than your child. Listen calmly as your children recount an occurrence and express whatever fears or concerns they feel. Tell them that they have your support. Be empathetic and comforting. Help them to work through the pain and confusion in a reassuring way. If you allow them to move beyond the experience, without dwelling on it or suppressing it, your children should recover over time.

If You Are the Victim

Victims of crime need to understand that the loss of control and the strong emotions that follow are disorienting. Your normal coping mechanisms may not be adequate. If you need help, ask for it. This may involve someone staying with you or your going to another location for awhile. You might need help buying groceries, caring for pets, or for cleaning and maintenance tasks. You might benefit from a leave of absence from work or referrals to health care providers or counseling services. Short-term assistance and long-term support and understanding will enable you to put your life back in order and work toward self-empowerment. This will not happen overnight and you will need the involvement of others to get you there, but you can survive a crime and get your life back together.

Do not abdicate decisions to others during your recovery period. You do not need to be rescued or taken over by others no matter how genuine their concern. Making as many decisions about your daily life as possible will help you regain a sense of control. Try not to make any big life decisions, though, at this time.

You are not at your best until you have worked through recovery and you might be reacting impulsively to the stress of the crime. As you reorganize your life in the aftermath of the crime, you may need to make adjustments to your lifestyle. Carefully consider your alternatives before making a drastic change and understand your motivation and expected results.

There are things that you can do for yourself that will make you feel better, although it is okay to give yourself permission to feel badly about the crime and to talk to others about it. Regular exercise and a healthy diet, including vitamin and mineral supplements if you need them, can have positive effects on your body and mind.

You should also structure your time to help you plan and control your days, and be sure to include activities that you enjoy with family and friends. While you are trying to rebuild the normalcy of your life, it may help to maintain a journal. Writing out your feelings and events can be extremely beneficial and therapeutic in working past the crime and discovering your inner strength for coping and healing.

If you find you are slipping into self-destructive behavior patterns, using drugs or alcohol to numb the pain or help you to forget the crime, or if your thoughts are focused on dying or suicide, get professional help immediately. Mental health agencies within the community usually offer counseling services on a sliding-scale fee system based on your income and financial resources. If you feel that friends or family are not available or are unable to help you work through the distress of the crime, see if your employer offers counseling services or if your church or synagogue can provide free counseling services for you.

Victim Assistance

Victim assistance has many faces and includes the social support of family and friends, the criminal justice system, and specialized organizations that provide services to the victims of crime. You should check with law enforcement agencies in your area, your local district attorney's office, the phone directory under Victim Assistance, and your public library to find out what services are available where you live.

These organizations and offices offer emergency assistance to victims immediately after a crime, such as a rape crisis center. Some provide loans and shelter, for example, to help women who are the victims of domestic violence. They may be able to help victims get back stolen property or apply for compensation for the financial losses associated with a crime. They may provide advocates for the victims to inform them about court cases, accompany them to court, or counsel witnesses of homicide or the survivors of homicide victims. They may also provide information or training for victims to help them get back a sense of control or learn crime prevention techniques for the future.

In addition, there are several national resources for information on victim's rights and assistance:

Office for Victims of Crime Resource Center
U.S. Department of Justice
P.O. Box 6000
Rockville, MD 20850
800-627-6872

National Organization for Victim Assistance
1757 Park Road, N.W.
Washington, DC 20010
800-879-6682

National Association of Crime Victim Compensation Boards
P.O. Box 16003
Alexandria, VA 22302
703-370-2996

National Victim Center
2111 Wilson Blvd., Suite 300
Arlington, VA 22201
703-276-2880

The National Victim Center has an INFOLINK program that provides referral information about victim-assistance programs across the country. Call toll-free 800-FYI-CALL for information and to receive information bulletins. The bulletins may also be accessed on the Internet at the Web site address http://www.nvc.org.

Depending on the nature of the crime, you might also contact the local chapter of a national citizen's group, such as Mothers Against Drunk Driving or Parents of Murdered Children.

There are also two groups of particular interest to women because they deal with crimes where women and children are the most likely victims:

National Coalition Against Sexual Assault
125 North Enola Drive
Enola, PA 17025
717-728-9764

National Coalition Against Domestic Violence
P.O. Box 18749
Denver, CO 80218
303-839-1852

Your public library can give you information on other such organizations. These organizations provide support groups for survivors, encourage family members to get involved, and provide advice to victims and witnesses on their rights.

Key Points To Remember

- Help combat crime by reporting suspicious activities.
- If you witness a crime, contact the police and give details of what you observed.
- An accurate description can help police apprehend a suspect.
- Observe particulars about any vehicle used in a crime.
- Ask police for the report number and other information about a case so you can trace its progress through the investigative process.
- Insist that victims and witnesses are treated with sensitivity.

- A victim advocate can help the victim to navigate the legal system.
- All 50 states have legislated rights for victims, but they vary.
- Crime affects the victim in many ways—physically, emotionally, and financially.
- Most crime victims show the effects of trauma and it takes time to recover from the experience.
- Seek counseling to help you work through your feelings about the crime.
- Victims benefit from the ongoing concern and support of friends and relatives.
- When children are victimized, let them talk out their concerns and fears.
- There are several victim assistance organizations that provide needed services to the survivors of crime.

Practice Scenarios

What if...?

You see a man cutting across your neighbor's lawn carrying a TV set.

You hear shots and two men come out of the bank, jump in a car, and speed out of the lot.

As you return from a swim in the pool, you see a strange man and woman exiting your hotel room with your purse slung over her shoulder.

Your daughter tells you that the teenage boy down the block invites her to his fort to play, and he takes pictures of her with her clothes off.

A good friend is beaten and raped in the stairwell of her apartment building and she calls you in hysterics from her apartment.

Bibliography

Allen, Jennifer. "The Danger Years." *Life*, July 1995, pp. 40-54.

A Safe Trip Abroad. Washington, DC: Department of State Publication 10110, Bureau of Consular Affairs, September 1993.

"Auto Theft Awareness/Prevention Techniques" and "Auto Theft Alert!" *CAR Newsletter*, Winter 1995. Palm Beach, FL: Citizens for Auto-Theft Responsibility.

Awareness Suggestions. Frederick, MD: Frederick County Sheriff's Office.

Bart, Pauline B. and Patricia H. O'Brien. "Stopping Rape: Effective Avoidance Strategies." *Journal of Women in Culture and Society*, Vol. 10, No. 1, 1984, pp. 83-101.

Benedict, Helen. *Safe, Strong, and Streetwise: Sexual Safety at Home, On the Street, On Dates, On the Job, at Parties and More*. Boston: Joy Street Books/Little, Brown and Company, 1987.

Berger, Laurie. "Hotel Crime: Are You As Safe As You Think?" *Corporate Travel*, Vol. 8, No. 2, November 1992, pp. 26-30.

Biery, Ken D., Jr., and James L. Schaub. *Women and Children First: How to Avoid Crime*. Renton, WA: Win/Win Publications, 1992.

Bishop, Bob and Matt Thomas. *Protecting Children from Danger: Building Self-Reliance and Emergency Skills Without Fear*. Berkeley, CA: North Atlantic Books, 1993.

Borgeson, Lillian. "Women & Cars." *Vogue*, January 1994.

Breaking the Cycle of Violence: A Focus On Primary Prevention Efforts. The League of Women Voters of Minneapolis, April 1990.

Brennan, Patricia. "The Link Between TV and Violence." *The Washington Post TV Week*, January 8, 1995, pp. 6 and 48.

Brittsan, Allison and Clarene Shelley. *Surviving: A Guide for Victims, Families, Friends, and Professionals*. Lakewood, CO: Word Services, Inc., 1994.

Bromley, Max L. and Leonard Territo. *College Crime Prevention and Personal Safety Awareness*. Springfield, IL: Charles C Thomas Books, 1990.

Buss, Dale D. "Combating Crime." *Nation's Business*, March 1994, pp. 16-24.

Carjacking: Preventing The Crime. Columbus, OH: Ohio Crime Prevention Association.

Chez, Nancy. "Helping the Victim of Domestic Violence." *American Journal of Nursing*, July 1994, pp. 33-37.

Child Abuse. Rockville, MD: Substance Abuse and Mental Health Services Administration, DHHS Publication No. (ADM-92) 1974, 1992.

Clavin, Thomas. "The Silent Epidemic: Crime in Hospitals." *Good Housekeeping*, September 1994, pp. 258, 260-261.

Community Action. Information Packet. Washington, DC: National Crime Prevention Council, 1994.

Crime Resistance: A Way to Protect Your Family Against Crime. Washington, DC: Federal Bureau of Investigation, U.S. Department of Justice.

Criminal Victimization in the United States, 1994. Washington, DC: Bureau of Justice Statistics, U.S. Department of Justice, NCJ-162126, May 1997.

Davis, Ester Payne. *Crime Prevention Handbook: A Practical Handbook for Everyone*. Dayton, OH: P.P.I. Publishing, 1983.

de Becker, Gavin. *The Gift of Fear: Survival Signals That Protect Us from Violence*. New York: Little, Brown and Company, 1997.

Dixon, Jay R. *Personal Protection and Security: A Practical Guide*. Chicago: Nelson-Hall Inc., 1985.

Dobson, Terry with Judith Shepherd-Chow. *Safe and Alive: How to Protect Yourself, Your Family, and Your Property Against Violence*. Los Angeles: J.P. Tarcher, Inc., 1981.

Duff, Elizabeth. "Can Your Child Cope With Conflict?" *Working Mother*, March 1994.

Estrella, Manuel M. and Martin L. Forst. *The Family Guide to Crime Prevention*. New York: Beaufort Books, Inc., 1981.

Fein, Judith. *Exploding the Myth of Self-Defense: A Survival Guide for Every Woman*. Torrance Publishing, 1993.

Fein, Judith. *Are You a Target? A Guide to Self-Protection, Personal Safety, and Rape Prevention*. Belmont, CA: Wadsworth Publishing Company, 1981.

Fike, Richard A. *How to Keep from Being Robbed, Raped & Ripped Off. A Personal Crime Prevention Manual for You and Your Loved Ones*. Washington, DC: Acropolis Books Ltd., 1983.

Fontanarosa, Phil B. "The Unrelenting Epidemic of Violence in America: Truths and Consequences." *Journal of the American Medical Association*, Vol. 273, No. 22, June 14, 1995, pp. 1792-1793.

Gardner, Carol Brooks. "Safe Conduct: Women, Crime, and Self in Public Places." *Social Problems*, Vol. 37, No. 3, August 1990, pp. 311-328.

Get A Jump On Carjackers. Washington, DC: Bureau of Justice Assistance, Office of Justice Programs, U.S. Department of Justice.

Gilgun, Jane F., Kay Pranis, and Richard C. Ericson. *A Survey of Minnesota Prison Inmates: Risk and Protective Factors in Adolescence*. Minneapolis, MN: Minnesota Citizens Council on Crime and Justice, October 1994.

Green, R.R. *Rape: The New Attitude for Prevention*. Torrance, CA: Green Productions, 1986.

Griffith, Liddon R. *Mugging: You Can Protect Yourself*. Englewood Cliffs, NJ: Prentice-Hall, Inc., 1978.

Bibliography

Grimes, Colby. "101 Crime Fighters." *Woman's Day*, October 11, 1994, pp. 48, 50, 52, 62. (Sourceline, p. 170).

Gonzales, Randolph A. *Crime Prevention for Children: A Basic Guide for Parents in Developing A Personal Safety Program for Children*. Eurich, Gonzales and Associates, Inc., 1986.

Hazelwood, Robert R. and Joseph A. Harpold. "Rape: The Danger of Providing Confrontational Advice." *FBI Law Enforcement Bulletin*, June 1986, pp. 1-5.

Hechinger, Grace. *How to Raise a Street Smart Child: The Complete Parent's Guide to Safety on the Street and at Home*. New York: Facts on File Publications, 1984.

Hersh, Kathy Barber. *Protect Yourself From Crime*. Boca Raton, FL: Globe Communications Corp., 1994.

Home Defense/Personal Security. Los Angeles, CA: Petersen Publishing Company, 1994.

Home Security. Information Packet. Washington, DC: National Crime Prevention Council, 1994.

How To Prevent Motor Vehicle Theft. Woodstock, MD: Maryland Community Crime Prevention Institute, Police Training Commission, Department of Public Safety and Correctional Services.

How To Protect You & Your Car. Washington, DC: American Association of Retired Persons, 1986.

"How To Protect Yourself From Crime." *The Lipman Report*, November 15, 1993. Memphis, TN: Guardsmark, Inc.

How To Report Suspicious Activities. Washington, DC: American Association of Retired Persons, 1986.

Huchton, Laura M. *Protect Your Child: A Parent's Safeguard Against Child Abduction and Sexual Abuse*. Englewood Cliffs, NJ: Prentice-Hall, Inc., 1985.

Hull, Karla. *Safe Passages: A Guide for Teaching Children Personal Safety.* Dawn Sign Press, 1986.

Involving Youth in Violence Prevention. Information Packet. Washington, DC: National Crime Prevention Council, 1993.

Johnson, Constance. "Silent Victims Who Witness Violence." *U.S. News and World Report*, March 27, 1995, pp. 29-30.

Johnson, Ray with Carroll Stoianoff. *Ray Johnson's Total Security: How You Can Protect Yourself From Crime.* New York: New American Library, 1985.

Jones, Richard O. *Tips Against Crime Written from Prison: A Crime Survival Guide for the '90s.* Sandcastle Publishing, 1993.

Kinkle, Susan L. "Violence in the Emergency Department: How to Stop It Before It Starts." *American Journal of Nursing*, July 1993, pp. 22-24.

Koumanelis, Samantha. *More Power To You! The Personal Protection Handbook for Women.* Ridgefield, CT: Round Lake Publishing Co., 1993.

Krulewitz, Judith E. and Arnold S. Kahn. "Preferences for Rape Reduction Strategies." *Psychology of Women Quarterly*, Vol. 7, No. 4, Summer 1983, pp. 301-312.

Learning About Conflict Management. Information Packet. Washington, DC: National Crime Prevention Council, 1993.

Lee, Eliot. "Body and Mind: Principles of Aikido Can Be Valuable in Police Work." *Police*, August 1991, pp. 36-38.

Lucas, Warren J. *Protection Made Easy.* Falls Church, VA: C & L Publishing Company, 1981.

Mann, Stephanie with M.C. Blakeman. *Safe Homes, Safe Neighborhoods.* Berkeley, CA: Nolo Press, 1993.

McGurn, Thomas P. with Christine N. Kelly. *The Woman's Bible for Survival in a Violent Society.* New York: Stein and Day/Publishers, 1984.

McKinley, Sarah, Sunny Graff, Elaine McCrate, and staff of Community Action Strategies to Stop Rape. *Fighting Back: A Self-Defense Handbook.* Columbus, OH: Women Against Rape, 1977.

McNamara, Joseph D. *Safe & Sane: The Sensible Way to Protect Yourself, Your Loved Ones, Your Property and Possessions.* A Robert Wool Book. New York: Perigee Books/The Putman Publishing Group, 1984.

Michelmore, Peter. "Riding With the Cellular Posse." *Reader's Digest*, October 1994, pp. 84-88.

Miltenberger, Raymond G. and Ellyn Thiesse-Duffy. "Evaluation of Home-Based Programs for Teaching Personal Safety Skills to Children." *Journal of Applied Behavior Analysis*, Number 1, Spring 1988, pp. 81-87.

Moyers, Bill. "What We Can Do About Violence." *Parade Magazine*, January 8, 1995, pp. 4-6.

Neighborhood Watch. Information Packet. Washington, DC: National Crime Prevention Council, 1994.

O'Block, Robert L., Joseph F. Donnermeyer, and Stephen E. Doeren. *Security and Crime Prevention.* St. Louis, MO: The C.V. Mosby Company, 1981.

On Guard! A Citizen's Crime Prevention Handbook. Denver, CO: Protection Unlimited, 1981.

Outsmarting Crime: A Personal Guide to Safer Living. Woodstock, MD: Maryland Community Crime Prevention Institute, Police Training Commission, Department of Public Safety and Correctional Services.

Padgett, Nina. "Going On Guard! Protecting Yourself Against Car Thieves." *RoadSmart*, Vol. 30, No. 2, Summer 1995, p. 16.

Personal Safety: Your Guide to Crime & Accident Prevention. Emmaus, PA: Rodale Press, Inc., 1995.

Protecting Children. Information Packet. Washington, DC: National Crime Prevention Council, 1994.

Quigley, Paxton. *Not An Easy Target*. New York: Fireside/Simon & Schuster, 1995.

"Real Estate Safety Precautions." *Real Estate Today*, Vol. 24, No. 8, p. 16(2).

Sabadini, Lou. *How To Be Crime Free*. Miami, FL: National Association of Chiefs of Police, 1989.

Safe & Secure Living: A Consumer's Guide to Home, Auto, and Personal Security. Vol. 2, No. 4, May 1994. Canoga Park, CA: Challenge Publications, Inc.

Singer, Mark I., Trina Menden Anglin, Li yu Song, and Lisa Lunghofer. "Adolescents' Exposure to Violence and Associated Symptoms of Psychological Trauma." *Journal of the American Medical Association*, Vol. 273, No. 6, February 8, 1995, pp. 477-482.

Serwer, Andrew E. "Crime Stoppers Make A Killing" *Fortune*, April 4, 1994, pp. 109-111.

Sexual Assault Prevention. Information Packet. Washington, DC: National Crime Prevention Council, 1994.

Sexual Assault Prevention Handbook. Crime Prevention Center, California Office of the Attorney General, Summer 1989.

Shuker-Haines, Frances. *Everything You Need to Know About Date Rape*. New York: The Rosen Publishing Group, 1990.

Simmons, J.L. and George McCall. *76 Ways to Protect Your Child From Crime*. New York: Henry Holt and Company, 1992.

State Farm Safe Home Guide. Bloomington, IL: State Farm Fire and Casualty Company.

Street Smart, Street Safe. Mace Security International, Inc., 1991.

Sussman, Vic. "A Can of Self-Defense." *U.S. News and World Report*, September 28, 1992, pp. 82 and 86.

Schwartz, John. "Statistics on Crimes Against Women Are Engulfed by Political Fog." *The Washington Post*, March 27, 1995, p. A4.

Talking With Youth About Prevention: A Guide for Law Enforcement and Others. Washington, DC: National Crime Prevention Council, 1992.

Talley, Larry. *Are You Really Safe? Protecting Yourself in America Today*. Marietta, GA: Longstreet Press, Inc., 1994.

Tatam, Robert. *Contra Costa County Crime Prevention Manual*. Concord, CA: Criminal Justice Agency and Crime Prevention Committee of Contra Costa County, 1977.

The Adventures of Surelocked Homes: Making Entry Less Elementary. Bloomington, IL: State Farm Fire and Casualty Company.

Travel Tips for Older Americans. Washington, DC: Department of State Publication 9309, Bureau of Consular Affairs, October 1989.

Tuten, Lisa, as told to Ellen Sherman. "I Was Stalked." *McCall's*, August 1995, pp. 55, 57, 59.

Williams, Terry, Eloise Dunlap, Bruce D. Johnson, and Ansley Hamid. "Personal Safety in Dangerous Places." *Journal of Contemporary Ethnography*, Vol. 21, No. 3, October 1992, pp. 343-374.

When a Child Reports a Crime: Encouraging Children To Report Crimes and Responding Appropriately When They Do. Washington, DC: National Crime Prevention Council, 1992.

Wilson, Michele D. and Alain Joffe. "Contempo 1995: Adolescent Medicine." *Journal of the American Medical Association*, Vol. 273, No. 21, June 7, 1995, pp. 1657-1659.

Wiseman, Rosalind. *Defending Ourselves: A Guide to Prevention, Self-Defense, and Recovery from Rape*. New York: The Noonday Press/Farrar, Straus and Giroux, 1994.

"Youth Health Still Declining In America, Study Says." *New York Times*, June 7, 1995, p. B10.

Index

Index

Ordering Information

Did you find useful information in this book? Would you like to share a copy with your wife, husband, child, parent, friend, employee, or college coed?

Individual copies may be ordered by sending $24.95 plus $3.50 shipping and handling to:

Foundation for Crime Prevention Education
113 North Washington Street, No. 217
Rockville, MD 20850

Or order by calling:

(toll free) **800-CRIME-RX** or **800-274-6379**

Please have your MasterCard or Visa ready.

Also, please note that quantity discounts are available on bulk purchases to police departments, local governments, colleges and universities, women's or safety groups, corporations, associations, and other groups for educational purposes or fund raising. Book excerpts or specially adapted booklets also can be developed for your particular needs.

Speakers from the Foundation are available for presentations on crime and safety issues. Please contact the Foundation at the above address.

About the Foundation

The Foundation for Crime Prevention Education was founded out of concern about the devastating effects that crime and violence have had on American families and neighborhoods. The mission of the Foundation is to develop public education projects and campaigns on important safety topics, emphasizing the ways that improved knowledge can prevent crime and victimization. Knowledge is power.

A Note to Readers

Do you know any proven personal safety methods and ideas that you have not seen in this book? Would you like to share them with others?

The Foundation has made every effort to research and present the most effective safety tips available. However, if readers of this book have discovered other great personal safety ideas, we would like to know about them.

We are interested in any methods that contribute to people's personal safety for consideration in future editions of this book and other information materials from the Foundation. If your personal safety tip has not been written about before and we use it in a later publication, the Foundation will gladly acknowledge your contribution.

If you will share your ideas or methods with us, please write to us (we must keep a written record) at:

Foundation for Crime Prevention Education
113 North Washington Street, No. 217
Rockville, MD 20850

You may also send us general comments about the book, and real-life examples of how the information in the book has helped you to live a safer life and avoid or deter crime.